Tammy is a retired registered nurse, who, after leaving nursing to raise her two children, found herself propelled onto a spiritual journey with a simple request from a friend to read the book *'Conversations with God'* by Neale Donald Walsch. Many years and many books later, the perception changing insights and invaluable information she received regarding the meaning of life, why we're here on Earth, and how to be happy by becoming aware of and embracing her true self were so life changing for her that she decided to open a small bookstore to share the amazing books that had transformed her life. She then became a certified self-empowerment life coach. Tammy lives with her husband, Bruce, in Grandview Heights, Ohio.

This book is dedicated to my husband, Bruce, whose love was, and is, the soil for my growth. Thank you for the countless hours you spent listening, questioning, challenging, and supporting me and my ever-evolving perceptions. I know that wasn't always easy. I love you.

Tammy Fleishman

BECOME YOURSELF

The Evolution of Feeling Good

AUSTIN MACAULEY PUBLISHERS™

LONDON • CAMBRIDGE • NEW YORK • SHARJAH

A CIP catalogue record for this title is available from the British Library.

ISBN 9781035808274 (Paperback)
ISBN 9781035808281 (ePub e-book)

www.austinmacauley.com

First Published 2023
Austin Macauley Publishers Ltd®
1 Canada Square
Canary Wharf
London
E14 5AA

As this book is, in large part, the story of my transformation, I first want to thank the people who went on this journey with me, allowing me to develop my newfound insights and perceptions. I changed so much during this time of my life that my good friend, John, told me he thought I had multiple soul personality disorder. Gratitude and deep appreciation to: my husband, Bruce Fleishman; my daughter, Rachael Radel; my son, Nic Radel; my step-daughter and son-in-law Amy and Gregg Robinson; my step-daughter and son-in-law Lauren and Chris Wager; friends Nancy Vogel, Joyce Shively, Kim Little, and Michele Zimmer. Thank you for listening and being fellow sojourners. To my life coaching clients, thank you for sharing your lives with me. Tanya Blair, you giving me a deadline was exactly what I needed. Thank you. I appreciate and value the feedback from those who read my manuscript, my beta testers: Bruce Fleishman, Rachael Radel, Nic Radel, Amy Robinson, (brother and sister-in-law) Dale and Penny Hart, (parents) Red and Doris Hart, Trish Brown, Peter and Gwen Gesler, Mary Loe, Nathan and Elisha Stanton, Travis Thiel, Alexis Yamokoski, and Michele Zimmer. Your input and inspiration meant the world to me. Peter Gesler, thank you for informing me about Reedsy, an on-line support site for authors. Reedsy gave me a place to start the process of publication when I had no idea how to go about getting a book published. Jennifer Capello, my Reedsy editor, was overwhelmingly beneficial in bringing Become Yourself to a mature and professional rendition. Jennifer, your expertise and observations made the book what it has become. Thank you.

Table of Contents

"The unexamined life is not worth living."

– Socrates

Introduction

Do dogs like bones?

No. They like steak. They settle for bones.

A few months ago, I was enjoying a cocktail after golf when a friend sat down to chat. This young man has a successful career, is attractive, has a beautiful wife, and had just welcomed a precious baby girl into his family.
He said to me, "I should be happy, but I'm not."
While he loved his family and career, he wasn't feeling a deep sense of fulfillment and wholeness. Something was missing.

I was not shocked. Clients came to my coaching business because they were anywhere from dissatisfied to miserable. These middle- to upper-class men and women were emotionally surviving instead of thriving. They were bored, dismayed, and depressed. There was no passion or enthusiasm, and little joy in their lives. Like dogs settling for bones, too many of us are way too willing to put up with these negative emotions, so I admired their unwillingness to do so.
At our first life coaching session, I would ask my clients these two questions:

"How in charge of your life do you feel?"

"For what purpose do you get out of bed in the morning?"

To the first question, I got answers that ranged from negative 150% to 40%. These people had families, careers, good health, friends – abundance in many ways. Yet they did not feel like they were able to make themselves happy. They felt disempowered and victimized.

Answers to the second question were, "I wish I knew." "Because I have to." "Nothing." "I have to work." "I have responsibilities." But far and away the most common answer to the question of what got them out of bed in the morning was, "To let the dogs out." Again, having most of the things that are supposed to make us happy, they had no 'feel good' reason to get out of bed in the morning.

Everyone wants to be happy. Over two thousand years ago, Aristotle concluded that, more than anything, men and women seek happiness. We seek health, wealth, adventure, relationships—literally everything—because we believe we will feel better by having or doing certain things. We all want to feel good. As psychoneuroimmunologist[1] Dr. Candace Pert said in her book, 'Everything You Need to Know to Feel Go(o)d', "If a plant growing in the rainforest in Brazil made people angry when they ingested it, no one would try to smuggle it into the country and sell it for recreational use. The plants that get cultivated are the ones that make us feel good."

When John Lennon was a young boy, his mom told him that the key to life was happiness. So, when a teacher gave him the assignment of writing about what he wanted to be when he grew up, he wrote that he wanted to be happy. The

---

[1] Psychoneuroimmunology is the study of how the mind communicates with the body.

teacher told him that she didn't think he understood the assignment. He told her he didn't think she understood life.

The founding fathers of the United States of America considered the pursuit of happiness an unalienable right endowed upon us by our Creator, just as important as life itself.[2]

If happiness—and what I mean by happiness is a feeling of deep contentment, fulfillment, and wholeness—is what we want and have sought through relationships, religion, money, helping others, looking good, acquiring things, vices—the list is endless—why do so many of us feel like something is missing? Why is it that we eventually get to that question, "Is this all there is?"

One major reason is that as young children wanting to be happy, we were highly influenced by the expectations, opinions, judgments, and actions of the people in our lives because happiness at that age came through acceptance. Comedian Kevin Hart says, "Acceptance is a drug as addictive as crack." What we wanted more than anything was to not be rejected. So, for reasons we will go into in detail in chapter three, we unconsciously traded authenticity for security. Unknowingly is the key here. We're not aware at that young age that we do this. We'll also delve deep into the ramifications of this later, but suffice it to say here, sooner or later in life we long for those missing pieces of ourselves. Except we don't know that. All we know is that something is missing. And despite all the good things in our lives, we aren't happy.

---

[2] Declaration of Independence, National Archives – Washington, DC.

The Aboriginal people of Australia have a tradition. When they meet, they look each other in the eye and ask, "Are you in there?" to which the reply is, "I'm here." It's a call to the true self to emerge and be known. Becoming yourself is getting back in touch with those aspects of yourself you never knew you abandoned. Without that connection and embracement, no matter how many wonderful people and things you have in your life, something will be missing, keeping you from the happiness, fulfillment, and empowerment that only comes from being authentically you.

The book 'Path of Empowerment' by Barbara Marciniak tells us, "Self-empowerment is the most natural and treasured flowing of an awakened mind. When you seek self-empowerment, you truly begin to live." It also says, "In order to empower your life you must first examine it." Self-empowerment starts with self-awareness. It is imperative that we become aware of what has been limiting us. It is life-changing and empowering to become aware of our natural and authentic desires – to what would bring us pleasure, purpose, and deep contentment. Truly, the unexamined life is not worth living. It's a journey that mankind has been undertaking even before Socrates wrote that quote. In his book 'Walking Between the Worlds', Gregg Braden shares, "The essence of becoming is the essence of the most sacred of the ancient texts." In her book 'Believe, Ask, Act', Mary Ann Dimarco says, "Authenticity is essential for the discovery of truth and for finding meaning and fulfillment. Authenticity is a spiritual priority." Authenticity is essential for self-empowerment.

My definition of a spiritual journey is a journey of expanded awareness, of evolving through learning. When we become more conscious, or aware, of who we really are, it's a whole new level of happiness. Aristotle used the term 'eudaimonia' for happiness. Its actual meaning is 'human flourishing'. We simply cannot flourish until we know ourselves as our authentic desires, bents, and beliefs, rather than those we unconsciously chose as children to avoid rejection. We need to find out who let those dogs out.

"Become Yourself" is the story of how I became myself. It is my experience of the transformational journey, from the despair and angst of the feeling that something was missing, to days filled with passion, meaning, and fulfillment. C. S. Lewis has this to say about experience: "What I like about experience is that it is such an honest thing." I believe that words alone don't teach. But in telling the stories of what I regard as the 'cool, weird'[3] experiences, guidance, and aha moments I had on my way to becoming myself, perhaps they can be a road map of sorts for others to do the same. And not only a road map – a short-cut. The very first self-help book I ever read was one that I read while going through my divorce. It was 'The Road Less Traveled' by M. Scott Peck. The opening line is, "Life is difficult." And I couldn't agree more. I was given the gifts of the time and support I needed to learn that my happiness and, therefore, wholeness needed to come from inside myself, and then figure out how to make that happen. Do I still have days where all I can think is, "Life is difficult?" Absolutely. I wrote this book so others like me wouldn't have to spend years, like I did, finding the way to get happy from the inside out. I wrote this book because I know first-hand the gnawing, depressing feeling of 'Is this all

---

[3] 'Weird' comes from an old Anglo-Saxon word meaning 'spiritual' and 'related to fate'.

there is?' I wrote it because my successful, seemingly thriving life coaching clients didn't have a reason to get out of bed in the morning. I wrote it because I wanted to share the practical techniques and processes I found and developed (and constantly go back to) that actually work to bring people back to themselves, put them back in charge of their lives, and infuse them with joy. And if I'm being perfectly honest, I wrote it because my dear friend Tanya gave me a deadline.

Chapter 1
The Student Begins

The student begins by asking the question, Who am I?
 – Bhagavan Sri Ramana Maharshi, Indian Hindu Sage

SOME YEARS BACK, comedian Phil Hartman did a skit on Saturday Night Live in which he played an impossible-to-please acting instructor whose students were scared and in awe of at the same time. The skit went like this: Acting student Troy was asked by Phil what he was working on. "Aladdin," said Troy.

"Good," answered Phil, "now get up there!"

Troy quickly jumped to the stage and started doing Aladdin. Phil yelled, "STOP!" and asked, "who are you?"

"I'm Aladdin?" queried Troy.

"I don't know, are you?" asked Phil.

"I AM!" declared Troy.

"No, you're not!" exclaimed Phil.

"You're Troy!"

"I'm Troy?" a puzzled Troy asked back.

Phil turned to the class and asked student Kelly, "Kelly, who is he?"

Kelly quickly responded, "Aladdin!—(no)Troy!—(no)Aladdin!"

"Shut up, you're not listening," Phil barked.

"Brian, who is he?"

"Troy!—(no)Aladdin!—(no)Troy!"

"Yes, good," said Phil, "Troy, sit down."

Funny skit. Not so fun in life when we let others decide who we are. Yet, it's almost like throughout our lives we've been in acting class, trying on different roles and changing those roles based on outside opinions and expectations of what we're supposed to be, want, and of what would make us happy. This works for a while. It works until we admit to ourselves that we really aren't truly happy. That something is missing. That's when, as the Sri Ramana Maharshi says, "The student begins."

As a young girl I purchased a small wooden plaque with this quote burned into it:

"Hide not thy talents for what were they made? What's a sundial in the shade?"

I kept this plaque well into adulthood. It spoke to me deeply. It said to me, "Live your purpose." It said, "Get out there and do your thing." It said, "Who I am has a lot to do with my purpose in life."

In his book 'Man's Search for Meaning', Viktor Frankl takes the position that a person finds happiness through having a 'why' to be here. His logo therapy is based on the premise that you cure the soul by leading it to find meaning in life. He believed that happiness was not to be pursued but that it must ensue from meaning. In a TEDx podcast about near-death experiences, Dr. Nicholas Kardaras tells of how growing up well-to-do left him with a sense of meaninglessness and emptiness. He became addicted to drugs, overdosed, and died. He came back to life driven to help others with addiction. He emphasizes in his talk how his feelings of having no purpose led him to drugs. Rabbi Steve Leder in his book 'The Beauty of What Remains', a book about coping with the death of a loved one, shares this thought: "I do not know that any of us could go on without seeking and finding some order, some meaning and purpose to life." People derive meaning from two beliefs: 1. Life has meaning 2. My life has meaning. Meaning is incomparably significant to happiness.

Early in my life, I found meaning through the purposes of being a student and active participant in sports, cheerleading, the band, my family and friends, and having a boyfriend. Later on, meaning came through my career, marriage, children, and remarriage. There was always the next milestone to achieve. But once I had achieved them all, something was still missing. I was thirty-three years old, happily married (this time), had the children I had always wanted, lived in a beautiful home in a quaint little neighborhood, and was fortunate to be a stay-at-home mom, which was my dream. I had the proverbial 'All." Except I didn't.

I was in the shade. I can't say I was clinically depressed. To quote a comedian I once heard, I was more like chronically disappointed. I loved and embraced my roles as a mom and wife and all the other hats I wore, but every day at 4:00, when all the to-dos were done, I was bored. Is this all there is? Am I supposed to raise good kids so they can raise good kids so they can raise good kids? Why should I make my bed every day just to sleep in it and remake it again EVERY DAY? The mundaneness and repetitiveness of daily life were really getting me down. Boredom inevitably spiraled down into angst and constant yearning for what was missing.

I am reminded of this paragraph from the book Atlas Shrugged:

> "She lighted cigarettes for an instant's illusion of purposeful action and discarded them within another instant, feeling the weary distaste of a substitute purpose. She looked at the room like a restless beggar, pleading with the physical objects to give her a motive, wishing she could find something to clean, to mend, to polish – while knowing that no task was worth the effort. When nothing seems worth the effort, it's a screen hiding a wish that's worth too much. What do you want?"

A waitress once asked the Dalai Lama the secret to life. He answered that it was happiness. "But," he said, "that's the easy question. The hard question is, 'What makes you happy?'"

I was happy with all the relationships I had – my husband, children, extended family, and friends. I was happy with the things I had – a beautiful home, no financial stress, poker group, soccer, being involved in my kids' school and sports, vacations, etc. And when I first started asking myself, "Is this all there is?" I put more expectations on those people and things to fill that void. "Make me happy!" "Be more, be better, be different, be my everything!" I don't think I am alone in falling into that trap. But it only leads to blaming others for not delivering on something that never should have been asked of them in the first place. Giving the responsibility for our deep satisfaction, joy, and contentment to the people and situations in our lives leaves us feeling like a victim when that impossible feat cannot be achieved. It drives a huge wedge between us and those we love and are loved by, and toxic, damaging resentment sets in.

Thankfully for me, one day the powerful thought came: what I wanted, what was missing from my life, what the source of my unhappiness was, wasn't more from the relationships and lifestyle I already had. It was a sense of personal purpose. I didn't have one and had no idea what it could be. Hide not thy talents…what were my talents? What's a sundial in the shade? My question was more like, "Why would a sundial be in the shade?" Answer: "Because it doesn't know it's a sundial! I was having a personal identity crisis. Who was I outside of my roles and relationships? What was my purpose here on Earth?"

I hadn't a clue.

Chapter 2
Just Do the Next Joyful Thing

What makes you happy makes you whole.
— Brené Brown, PhD, MSW

ACCORDING TO MY self-diagnosis, my life was missing a personal purpose and that was the source of my angst. At the time, I thought of that purpose as an assignment of sorts. Something in particular I was supposed to be doing. A destiny, if you will. As determined as I was to figure out what, exactly, that purpose was, searching myself and seeking desperately, I wasn't coming up with any answers. This was driving me further and further into frustration and daily disappointment. Realizing I needed help discovering this illusive personal purpose, I knew one thing. Well, I knew two things. I knew I needed help and that I wanted that insight to come from someone who looked at life differently. I decided to ask a psychic what my purpose was. Surely a psychic would be able to look into the ether and give me the guidance I wasn't able to find on my own.

I made an appointment, and the anticipation of waiting for it was killing me and thrilling me all at the same time. But I had been to see this psychic before and he had given me accurate and helpful information, so I was overjoyed to have this opportunity again. Finally, the day arrived. The time had come. I was going to find out my personal purpose. The thing that was going to catapult me out of gloom and into passion was so close! Sitting in the chair across from the psychic, I begged him to "PLEASE just tell me what it is I'm supposed to be doing. I can do anything! Just tell me what it is!"

The psychic looked at me very calmly and said, "Oh. That's easy. Just do the next joyful thing. That will lead you to your passion, which will lead you to your purpose."

Um, WHAT? That wasn't even psychic!

Talk about disappointed. I was utterly deflated. Back at square one. I went through my days doing what needed to be done. Nothing had changed. One day, feeling that mundaneness that led to boredom and then depression setting in once again, I decided there was nothing left to do except follow the psychic's advice. I made up my mind to just do the next joyful thing. I thought to myself, *What is it that I could do that would keep me interested and jazzed and would make me lose all track of time because I would be so absorbed in it? What really, really floats my boat?* My answer was to go to the bookstore and buy a book about the meaning of life, why we're here, and what it's all about. When I was around five years old, I called my mom into my bedroom to ask her if she would make my tombstone now so I could see it before I died. I had been lying in bed pondering never having been born. I couldn't wrap my head around never having existed. I guess I figured seeing my tombstone would remedy that! My mom is a very practical woman of German descent, but that was a bit too practical even for her. She declined. Lovingly. But I really don't remember thinking too much about life and

24

existence after that. Perhaps it was because I started going to church and accepted the Judeo-Christian philosophies on life and why we're here. But now, feeling the mundaneness and boredom of 'there's got to be more to life than this', I was once again deeply intrigued and curious about this thing we call life.

I wasn't sure how doing something I was passionate about would lead me to knowing who I am, why I'm here, and how I should live my purpose. Was reading my purpose? I thought not. But it felt good to have something to do that I truly enjoyed. Each and every time I felt bored, I would go buy another book. To say I devoured those books is a gross understatement. I couldn't wait to get out of bed every morning and read. Finding myself still in my pajamas on the couch reading at 2:30 in the afternoon, having shirked the house cleaning, laundry, and other responsibilities I had, I would have to rush to get dressed to pick up the kids from school. I simply could not get enough. I took copious notes. Legal pads and Bic pens became annual Christmas gifts from my husband to restock my supply. New ideas flowed. My perceptions and premises changed completely as I read and evolved. This was most definitely my passion. Born out of my next joyful thing of learning about why we're here on Earth.

One book led to another, and after eleven years of reading on my couch every spare minute I could steal, I opened a small bookstore. I wanted to share all the wonderful books that had changed my life. I named the store 'goodbooks' because every time I would finish a book, I would hold it to my chest and say out loud, "That was such a good book." Preparing for opening the store was truly my next joyful thing. I loved making lists of books to order. I spent many wonderful hours designing and decorating with a very good friend whom you'll meet later in the book. Once open, I was elated each and every time a customer would come in, browse, spend time in the window seats, and (of course) buy a book. Having the bookstore brought even more mind-opening books and experiences into my life.

One morning, I was at home looking through some books I had ordered for the store.

Before my husband left for work, I said to him, "Ya know, I've read so many different authors and they each offer a different perspective on life, but I bet they don't read each other's books. I think I'll write a book that puts together all these different viewpoints and call it Make the Connection."

About an hour later, my husband called me and said, "You're not going to believe it. I just got out of a meeting and the meeting was called 'Make the Connection'."

This was one of those 'cool, weird' experiences I spoke of in the introduction. I felt hugged by the Universe. I felt connected. I felt heard and acknowledged. And I also thought it was pretty humorous of the Universe to connect to me through the phrase 'make the connection'. I have not written the book yet, but this experience enlightened me even further to the Network we all belong to.

Another time, a woman came into the store and fell in love. With the books. She raved and raved and was acquiring quite a nice stack of books to purchase. She was so excited that she decided she just had to share this good news with her husband. She called him and very passionately expressed her joy in finding my store. I could hear the husband's response.

He said, "Honey, is your blood sugar getting low?" Immediately, this woman almost collapsed on my counter. I had to help her sit down and give her my banana from my lunch! She left without buying a thing. I was amazed at the power her husband's suggestion had over her. Here, right in front of me it seemed, was a living example of giving away our joy based on the opinion of another.

Around four o'clock one warm, sunny summer afternoon, three men wandered into the store. They wore paint-splotched white t-shirts and painter's pants, and they smelled of beer. I thought to myself, *These guys are in the wrong place. I'm sure they're not going to be interested in anything in here.*

Just then, one of the guys—with a very Southern drawl—asked, "Ya got any of them there Pema Chödrön books?"

Pema Chödrön is an American Tibetan Buddhist who teaches and writes about navigating life. Needless to say, I was shocked.

I answered, "No, I don't. But I should."

And then I admonished myself to not judge a book by its cover.

That lesson, however, needed to be presented to me more than once. And very literally! I had ordered a book called Radical Forgiveness for the store. When it came, I disliked the cover very much. So much so that I placed it on a high shelf and wouldn't even read it. Then, on one particularly slow day, I decided I was going to read the book, most likely was not going to like it, and would never order another one. That book, by author Colin Tipping, was foundational in changing my life views. It remains one of my all-time favorites. Don't judge a book by its cover. *Even bigger – don't judge. Got it.* (I think.)

While 'goodbooks' was long on good books and enlightening experiences that further aided my growth, it was short on longevity. I closed the bookstore after only two years so I could spend more time with my son during his senior-year of high school. My next joyful thing, building on all the insights, revelations, processes, and guidance I had received all those years of reading and growing in awareness on my couch and then in the bookstore, was to develop my own unique self-empowerment life coaching technique. I spent the next eleven years as a self-empowerment life coach. And now I'm writing this book. Just like the psychic said it would, doing the next joyful thing (and then the next joyful thing, etc.) led me to my passions, which led me to my purpose: sharing what I learn to help others find their happiness and peace through the self-empowerment that being our unique and authentic self can bring.

The psychic's advice was brilliant. It led me to find the answers inside. What made me joyful? Only I could know that. Only you can know that for yourself. American professor and author Joseph Campbell spent his career studying the triumph of the human spirit. He concluded the way was to follow your bliss.

He said, "If you do follow your bliss, you put yourself on a track that has been there for you all the while, waiting for you, and the life that you ought to be living is the one you are living…wherever you are. If you are following your bliss, you are enjoying the refreshment, that life within you, all the time."

My life coaching business was called Become Yourself. You might be thinking, *How can I not be myself?* Well, who do you know besides my psychic and Joseph Campbell that told you to just do what makes you happy? We're not trained that way. We deny, or never even consider, that part of ourselves. The advice to just do the next joyful thing in order to find my personal purpose seemed ludicrous to me. Now I know that those things I enjoy—and by 'enjoy'. I mean find interesting, intriguing, inspiring, fulfilling; things that raise my vibrations—are my guideposts to my purpose. My purpose wasn't assigned to me as I had formerly believed. It was within my joy.

After our first session of life coaching, I would give my clients the homework to just do the next joyful thing for the following week. A lot of them didn't know what made them joyful. One of the ways to tap into it is by remembering what you did as a child when you could do whatever you wanted. As a kid, I pretended to be a teacher. A lot. I would go to my school on the weekends and pretend I was the recess teacher, imaginary whistle in hand, imaginary high heels clicking and clacking as I walked the playground. At home, I made up Sunday school lessons with crafts that I would teach to my imaginary students. I loved it. The essence of being a teacher is learning, sharing what you know, and guiding. While for a career I became a nurse and not a professional teacher, my true nature is to learn and then share that knowledge with others.

One day, I was on an airplane and the woman sitting next to me was intrigued by what I was reading. I was reading about death and near-death experiences. This was interesting to my seatmate because she had lost her husband to cancer one year earlier and she herself had just finished chemotherapy. She had also just retired and was wondering what was next for her in life. What should she do with her time now? What was her next purpose? She was feeling directionless and that her life now had no meaning. I asked her what she did as a little girl when she could do whatever she wanted. She gave me an answer I got frequently from my clients. She said she played sports with the neighborhood kids. And then she, like my clients, said, "But I can't do that now." I asked her what was the essence behind the form of playing sports. While playing sports was what she was doing—what was it about playing sports that made her enjoy them—the essence behind the form? It could have been that she loved being a part of a shared sense of purpose. It could have been that she loved being creative in the sport and making things happen. We discussed several potential reasons why she liked sports, and what resonated with her was that she loved being a part of a shared sense of purpose. Her job had provided that for her before she retired. She had been thinking of traveling the world and doing charity work but didn't know which charities to trust. I just happened to have read a book called A Path Appears by Sheryl WuDunn and Nicholas Kristol. It's a book about the inside story of charities around the world. I shared this with her, and she lit up. She went from having a vague idea of what to do next with her life, to being excited and eager to check out this book and get started on her new path. So, if what thrilled and fulfilled you while growing up doesn't seem to fit your life now, look for the essence behind why you enjoyed it—the essence behind the form—and then follow your intuition on ways you can express that essence here and now.

Knowing what brings you joy is very much an intuitive process. After all, only you can know what truly makes you happy. For instance, somewhere inside you may have a vision or an inner knowing about yourself. From the time I can remember, I had a vision of myself sitting at a typewriter, glasses on, hair in a ponytail, cup of coffee at my side, writing. The typewriter has become a chrome book and I'm not a fan of ponytails (for me) anymore, but here I sit, coffee at my side, writing. While writing is my joy now, it came after years of reading, having a bookstore, and then being a self-empowerment coach. One passion led to the next. My life-long vision of myself as a writer couldn't happen for me until I had the experiences, knowledge, transformations, and stories about which to write. But I enjoyed each next joyful thing leading up to writing, and still do.

Another way to figure out your next joyful thing is to realize that you know what you want by what you don't want. Dislike being indoors? Your next joyful thing (NJT) will probably be an outside venture. Don't care for conforming? Your NJT may be about creating and owning your own style and approach. In my case, I did not like not knowing why we're here and what life is all about, so, therefore, I knew I wanted to know that. Once you know what you don't want, run some options for what you do want across your intuition. If something raises your vibrations—makes you excited, sounds really interesting, can't wait to get started—you've found your next joyful thing. In her book 'Dying to Be Me', Anita Morrjani shares her near-death experience. While she was on the other side, clinically dead here on Earth, she was shown how she had given up herself by trying to please everyone else in her life. She said, "I feel like when we say someone is of a higher vibration, we probably mean they are letting more of their authentic magnificence through." I became truer to myself and more of my true self by doing what raised my vibrations – the next joyful thing.

You may be thinking that it's too late, that you already have a career or a job whether you like it or not. Personal purposes do not have to become your career or be within your career. In time, they might be, but they can be hobbies and ways to spend your life in addition to your job. Professor and researcher Dr. Brené Brown tells of a rabbi who is also a rapper and an accountant whose joy is making jewelry. And as Dr. Brown says, "What makes you happy, makes you whole."

Become Yourself

- Just do the next joyful thing.
  - You know what you want by what you don't want.
  - What's the essence behind the form?
  - Does it raise your vibrations?

Chapter 3
If It Bugs You, It's About You

We don't see things as they are, we see them as we are.

— Anais Nin

PICTURE, IF YOU will, a hand-held folding fan. I used these fans to illustrate to my clients that when they are doing their next joyful thing and feeling good and full of passion they are like a wide-open fan. Their vibrations are high, energy is flowing, they feel inspired, and they feel empowered. They're 'cooking with gas' as an old friend used to say. This is how I felt on my couch reading and learning and expanding. I was a wide-open fan. But at the beginning, when I was just starting to let myself do the next joyful thing, I struggled. I felt a lot of self-judgment for spending copious hours reading. Thoughts came to me like, Reading is such a lazy passion. Get up and clean. Get up and DO something! And I would feel my fan closing and my joy dissipating as I got up to do something.

I have a friend whose name is Travis Thiel. In high school, Travis was a talented wrestler. He was invited to compete in an invitational with hundreds of other wrestlers from across the country. He tells me this invitational continues to this day. This particular year, the matches were being held in a huge convention center. Mats were everywhere. When it came time for Travis's first match, this is what he heard over the loudspeaker, "On mat forty-two, Travis Thiel versus Travis Thiel."[4] First of all, what are the chances of that? But even more importantly, this is what we all do! We wrestle ourselves. Why do we do this? If all we want is to feel good and we're doing something that makes us feel good, why do we judge that thing or ourselves for doing it? Reading about life and why we're here was, hands down, the most fulfilling personal thing I could do with my free time at that point in my life. Why was I wrestling with myself about it?

As we touched on in the introduction, from birth to around age seven to nine we (nothing new here) wanted to feel good. At these vulnerable ages, feeling accepted was how we felt good. Our very survival depended on not being rejected by our tribe. We needed to be accepted by what I like to call the Ps in our lives: parents, peers, professors/teachers, preachers/priests, police. We learned that conforming to the Ps gained our acceptance and that made us feel secure and happy. As Paul Selig says in The Book of Freedom, we subconsciously, as young children, were asking ourselves, "Am I lovable? Am I enjoyable? Am I worth it? Am I wanted? Am I chosen? Am I sought?" And we looked to the Ps to find confirmation of those things. We learned to kind of please others as a way of pleasing ourselves. Of course, we weren't aware we were doing that. In fact, from ages zero to seven/nine we aren't fully conscious or aware. Our brains are under the influence of a brain wave state called 'theta' during

---

[4] The opponent spelled his last name differently, but phonetically it was pronounced the same.

these years. Theta brain waves put us in a state between consciousness and sub-consciousness. It's what makes us extremely imaginative and suggestive as kids. It's also the brain wave state of hypnosis. Theta waves create a state of mind unconstrained by logic.[5] As we unconsciously and without logic learned to mold ourselves to not be rejected by the Ps in our lives, we sort of hypnotized ourselves into that way of being. The Ps influenced us powerfully. We cared deeply about their opinions, both positive and negative. I'd like to share this story about the power of the Ps in our lives as we were growing up.

My good friends Poh and Tom were having me and some other friends over for dinner. I brought an apple pie and whipped cream for dessert. The whipped cream was in a bag and couldn't be seen. Tom and Poh's young daughter Grace, who was three or four years old at the time, ran out to meet me in the driveway.

I said, "Hi, Grace! Would you like to carry the apple pie?"

She answered, "No. But I'll carry the whipping cream."

I was very surprised she knew I had whipped cream in the bag.

We went inside and I said to Poh, "I think your daughter is psychic."

I went on to tell her the story of the whipped cream. We laughed and thought nothing more about it. A few minutes later, our friends John and Nicci came to the door. Grace greeted them as well.

John said, "Hi, Grace! How are you?"

---

[5] "The Body Keeps the Score" by Bessel Van Der Kolk, MD.

Grace beamed up at John with the energy and bubbliness of a happy little girl and excitedly said, "I'm..." at which point her face dropped, her voice and energy changed to dreariness, and she finished with '...sick'. She thought I had said to her mom that I thought Grace was sick when I said I thought she was psychic. She took my opinion over her own knowing that she felt great and wasn't sick at all.

Growing up we were taking our clues for how to be, fit in, and think about ourselves from outside ourselves. By doing this, we—at times—rejected or denied what innately and uniquely made us happy, made the opinions of others more important than our own, avoided behaviors and personality traits that might get us judged, and formed beliefs about ourselves based on what the adults in our lives said and did to us. We unconsciously decided it wasn't worth risking our acceptance, and subsequently our worth, to follow our own bliss unabashedly, be true to our feelings, and act out our natural personalities and bents. We also didn't have the where with all or maturity to not blame ourselves for the dysfunctional actions and words of the Ps. A very important point: this doesn't apply to everything we chose to do or not to do as a child. But it applied often. When I was playing imaginary teacher, I was very happy and acting only on what brought me joy. But let's say my parents didn't want me to become a teacher and discouraged my acting that out in my play. I would have felt their disapproval, possibly only have played teacher when my parents weren't around, and unconsciously formed a feeling that that part of me was unacceptable or not desirable. And since true self-worth comes from loving and finding joy in the whole of who we naturally and uniquely are and what we desire, we unknowingly gave over the decision of our value and worth to the opinion of others.

I would give my clients a card that read, "My sense of self-worth comes from _____." Clients filled in the blank with 'my mother', 'my career', 'my success', 'my weight', 'being a parent', etc. Only one time did someone say they got their sense of self-worth from themselves. And I get that. The dynamics of our theta state of mind coupled with our strong desire to be accepted made it easy for us to deny some of what would make us happy and fulfilled and not even realize we were doing it. Authentic self-worth must come from something that can neither be added to nor taken away from you. Careers, success, your weight, being a parent – all these external things can and do change. Loving and owning all of your natural and unique desires, bents, opinions, and gifts, while they evolve as you do, is self-worth.

By the time we are okay with venturing outside our tribe, we've accumulated so many beliefs. Beliefs we don't know we have. Beliefs that worked for us when all we wanted was to be accepted. And that wasn't a bad thing. Actually, it really couldn't have been avoided. We look to the Ps for validation, approval, confirmation, lovability, and worth. I watch my grandkids vying for the attention, acceptance, and praise of their parents all the time.

"Watch me, Mom!" "Look what I can do, Dad!" "Watch me, watch me, watch me!" They salivate to hear their parents say, "Good job! Look at you!" They thrive on their parents' acknowledgment. When our parents (and the rest of the Ps in our lives) praised us, we internalized a feeling of worth from that praise. My 7-year-old grandson had a teacher who encouraged and employed the concept of a 'push' and a 'praise'. The idea is that as a teacher or parent you push the child to go beyond where they have gone before and when they do you praise them. I was doing this with my grandson in the swimming pool. I pushed him to swim farther than he ever had. He did.

For the praise part, I asked him, "Was that really fun?" He said to me, "That's not a praise. You're supposed to say 'I'm proud of you! That was awesome!'"

Children look externally for validation. They just do. As an adult, they continue looking outside themselves for validation and approval because they have a belief that without it, they're not deserving. Of course, the flip side is also true. If an all-powerful P disapproves of something a child does or enjoys, the child will form a belief regarding that disapproval. Beliefs like crying/expressing my emotions is not okay; it's not okay to take risks; being active is more valuable than reading. These beliefs worked for us as kids because they got us what we needed to feel good. They got us accepted. They formed a box we felt safe in. But when we reach a point in our lives when we're trying to decide what thrills and fulfills us these beliefs get in the way. They limit us and become what are called, well, 'limiting beliefs'. We find ourselves on mat forty-two, wrestling ourselves.

You might be thinking that if something is in your subconscious mind, like our beliefs, why worry about it? If it's subconscious, how can it be affecting my life? In his book The Exquisite Risk: Daring to Live an Authentic Life, Mark Napo says, "Our subconscious minds are not troublesome because of what remains suppressed. They are troublesome because they dominate what we express." I have read that our subconscious minds can process forty million neuronal impulses/second. Our conscious minds can process forty neuronal impulses/second. [6] The subconscious mind is powerful and is calling the shots until we bring those subconscious beliefs to our awareness. In 'Walking Between the Worlds', author Gregg Braden shares that the heart tells the brain what to do. The brain tells the body. What tells the heart? Your beliefs. Until you understand that you create everything with your beliefs, you are a victim of those beliefs. I'm reminded of a story about my friend Travis's little boy, Dylan. Dylan was sending his truck rolling over the top of his toy chest and crying uncontrollably every time the truck fell off the end of the chest. He did it over and over. He never put together that it was his action of rolling the truck across the toy chest that ultimately ended in the truck falling over the edge. If we never make the connection that a limiting belief is behind the troubling things occurring in our lives, those limiting beliefs will continue to rule our experiences.

The Ps have dominant influence over us as children. And those influences can become beliefs we hold about ourselves. Most of them serve us well. The limiting ones, however, are the ones that keep our vision boards from being realized, our desires unmet, and our affirmations ineffective. Limiting beliefs are the biggest contributing factor to us not becoming ourselves. They are the biggest reasons we close down our fans. Limiting beliefs—LBs—are like extra pounds that weigh us down. Just the other day I heard someone refer to these limiting beliefs as 'BS', which she said stands for 'Belief Systems'. I liked that. They are BS. They no longer

---

[6] "Spontaneous Evolution" by Bruce H. Lipton, PhD, and Steve Bhaerman.

empower us, but they are guiding our thoughts, feelings, and actions.

There comes a time in all our lives when we must become aware of and release those old beliefs. It's critical to becoming ourselves and the evolution of how to feel good. It is essential that we get our sense of worth and value from within, not from others. I call it the evolution of feeling good because we all start out getting our good feelings from outside ourselves and then must evolve to getting them from our own opinions of ourselves. Early on in my spiritual journey, I would read often something like the answers are all inside you. It used to frustrate me because no one ever told me how to find them. I was fortunate to be guided over the years of my journey to learn how to discover those answers from within. It started with becoming aware of and allowing myself my next joyful thing. The next step was learning that I had beliefs that were limiting my empowerment and how to bring those subconscious beliefs to my awareness.

The Healing Dimensions: Resolving Trauma in Bodymind and Spirit, is a book that deals with releasing past trauma. In it, author Brent Baum tells us, "Rule #1 is: Follow the emotion. It is the guide to bringing the subconscious to the conscious." Likewise, feelings are always the key to figuring out your limiting beliefs. In the book I am so very grateful I actually read and didn't discard based on its cover—Radical Forgiveness—Colin Tipping makes the statement, "If you want to know what you believe, look at what you have in your life. Your life always reflects your beliefs." The negative feelings we feel in our lives and relationships are like mirrors reflecting back to us the beliefs we need to look at and release so we can be that wide-open fan, feeling good, passionate, and

40

fulfilled. If it bugs you, it's about you. My self-judgment of reading all day came from within me. No one else in my present day life was judging me or telling me it was wrong. Experiences that trigger any negative emotion such as self-judgment, frustration, fear, hurt, shame, judgment of others, feeling patronized, unworthy, victimized—to name a few—are alerting you that you have a belief that is limiting you. If it bugs you, you can be sure there is a belief you don't know you have that is related to that thing that bugs you. Your soul is begging you to bring that belief to the surface so you can look at it and decide if it is still serving you or not. Trust me, it's not. Had I let my limiting belief that reading is a lazy passion win the wrestling match, I would have denied my passion and never have found my purpose.

We simply must become aware of our limiting beliefs and choose differently. Because this is so imperative to our empowerment and joy, I'd like to drive the point home even further by sharing some stories from my own life as examples of how these beliefs show up and negatively impact our happiness.

If you want to know what you believe, look at what you have in your life. Your life always reflects your beliefs.

If it bugs you, it's about you

I was in my late forties and had fallen in love with playing soccer. I played three days a week, and my good friend, Amy, played, too. It started to bug me that Amy had to fight for every 50/50 ball. She was relentless. She would do whatever it took to win that ball. I would think to myself, *Geez! It's old lady soccer on a Monday morning in Columbus, Ohio.* No one's getting paid here. It really got to me. It didn't bother any of the other players. They actually admired her tenacity and grit. This was my perception and mine alone. I was a life coach at this time and knew that since this was bugging me, it was about me. It was reflecting back to me something I needed to look at in myself. I knew it was about a belief I subconsciously had about myself that was limiting me. As the book *Transformation of the Species* points out, "Every time your buttons are pushed, you are looking in the mirror."

I wracked my brain to figure it out but to no avail. After all, I didn't feel the need to win every 50/50 ball. (I should add that I didn't have the ability, either. Amy did.) Then one day my husband Bruce and I were having a doozy of an argument. I wouldn't let up. After a while, a completely exasperated and frustrated Bruce slammed his fist down on the table and yelled, "TAMMY! Why do you ALWAYS have to win?"

Ding ding ding. There it was. I knew immediately why Amy's need to win every ball bugged me so much. Growing up, I was good in school. I won spelling bees, times tables races, and got all As. This pleased my parents and teachers greatly, which in turn made me feel worthy and good. It pleased me, too, but the praise and adulations I received validated me. It wasn't a negative thing that my parents and teachers were proud of me, but because at that young age I was looking outside of myself for approval, I developed a belief that Being right and winning academically made me valued, lovable, and worthy. That belief worked for me then. It gave me a feeling of worth. But fast forward to marriage where the need to be right so I could be valued, lovable, and worthy made me a b – well, let's just say it didn't make me very lovely to live with. And it was wreaking havoc in my marriage. Bruce never felt like he could be right or even understood. I so badly needed to be right because my subconscious belief dictated that was how I got love and worth. I couldn't understand how he didn't admire how smart and right I was! This old way of feeling good wasn't working anymore. This belief I had in the box of beliefs I had built around me growing up that kept me feeling safe and secure was now a barrier to my happiness. And my frustration and judgment surrounding this experience was showing me there was something in me that needed brought to my awareness. It wasn't about Amy at all. It was about releasing the need to be right in order to feel worthy and lovable.

In the above story, we see how a positive action by the Ps can still lead to forming a belief that no longer serves us later in life. Here is a story of a negative action and the belief that formed in my subconscious because of it.

I was around five or six years old. I was chubby but didn't know it. I loved myself! And I loved the little orange bikini I was wearing the day I was playing in my grandparents' front yard with my siblings and cousins. I grew up in Massillon, Ohio—home of the then infamous Massillon Tiger football team. The Tigers' theme song was, "Hold 'em, Tigers! Hold 'em Tigers!" On this day, with me rocking my orange bikini, my older cousin looked at me and sang, 'Oh fat Tammy! Oh fat Tammy!' to the tune of the Tiger theme song. I felt instant shame and rejection. In that very moment, I formed a subconscious belief that Being fat makes me unacceptable and unworthy. To this day I struggle with loving myself when I am seeing myself as fat. And I've suffered many unhappy times because of it. Even though I am aware of where this belief originated from, I have a hard time releasing it. I believe that limiting beliefs formed as a result of being shamed hold much power. There is no need for shame in this world. It is very damaging to a soul.

While most limiting beliefs are formed while growing up, through our interactions with the Ps, we can also form them in the womb and continue forming them even as adults.

Some years ago, I dragged Bruce to horse therapy. Wyatt Webb, author of 'It's Not About the Horse', was leading it. Its premise was that horses are perfect mirrors for us, reflecting back to us issues we have inside of us of which we are unaware. If a horse acted up or refused to act, it wasn't about the horse. It was about us. We were first asked to pick a horse in the corral. Using only our thoughts, energy, and touch, never speaking, we were supposed to get the horse to lift its leg for hoof cleaning, walk from one end of the corral to the other and back, and, finally, to let us stand directly in front of it and brush its face. Wyatt warned us that you can't schmooze a horse. He informed us that no manner of cajoling would get the horse to perform if our energy and intentions weren't clear and firm. He said, "Don't walk up to your horse and think—Oh, you're such a pretty horse—to get on its good side." He said, "Horses aren't people and they would see right through such inauthentic, manipulative energy." Even so, the first thing I thought as I was approaching my horse was, You're such a pretty horse. Busted. I immediately wondered how many times I had tried this with the people in my life. Nonetheless, things worked out well for Bruce and me in this part of the therapy. Next, the ten of us participating were led to a circular pen surrounded by bleachers. There was a horse inside the pen, and we were all outside on the bleachers. We were each supposed to take a turn inside the pen with the horse, getting the horse to walk, trot, and canter in one direction and then turn around and do the same in the other direction. Again, we weren't allowed to speak and could only use our thoughts, energy, and body language to get the horse to perform these tasks. We had a whip but were only allowed to hit the ground with it. The first two women whom Wyatt called on carried out the task perfectly.

I leaned over to Bruce and whispered, "I'm not doing this. It's obvious the horse already knows what to do. It doesn't matter who is in the ring."

The next thing I knew, Wyatt was pointing at me and saying, "You're next!"

I asked, "Why?"

He said, "Because I saw you lean over and tell your husband a story. I wonder if you'd be willing to stand up and share that story with the rest of us."

Busted again! I stood up and said I thought it didn't matter who was in the ring. I felt the horse was trained by doing the same thing over and over every day. He invited me into the ring, and I went. And he left. He had been in the ring with the first two ladies. *Whatever,* I thought. I took the whip and tried my best. I got the horse to do everything except canter in the opposite direction. Wyatt re-entered the ring and asked me how the experience made me feel. I said that it didn't make me feel anything.

I said, "You gave me a job to do, and I did it as best as I could."

He repeated, "How did it make you feel?"

I repeated, "It didn't."

Then he asked me, "How did you feel when I left the ring?"

I answered, "I figured you were just trying to set me up for failure because you being in the ring must be important."

His next question brought my husband leaping to his feet.

Wyatt asked me, "Why don't you trust men?"

Bruce was pumping his fist in the air and shouting, "She doesn't trust men!"

My reaction to Wyatt leaving me in the ring alone 'to set me up' was a mirror showing Wyatt that I didn't trust men. Wyatt explained that he left me in the ring by myself because he had seen me pick the biggest horse in the corral and get it to trust me enough to perform all the things I asked it to do. Not because he was trying to set me up for failure.

I told this story to my mom, and her response was that I had never trusted men. She said that, as a baby, if an uncle or any man would walk into the room where I was in my highchair, I would put my head down on the tray and not look up until that man had left the room. And if he didn't leave the room, I would fall asleep with my head on the tray. Somehow, I had formed a belief that men can't be trusted, but I had no clue whatsoever I had that belief. This unconscious belief gave me the thought that Wyatt was trying to set me up for failure, when, in actuality, he was trusting me to be alone in the ring. (I'm still not sure if I believe him!) More importantly, it made me question Bruce's decisions and actions frequently because, unknowingly, I didn't trust men.

Up next in the ring was Bruce. Poor Bruce. He whipped the ground repeatedly and emphatically. He ran to show the horse what he wanted it to do. But the horse barely moved. Try as he might, and he was trying mightily, sweating profusely, the horse mostly just looked at him as if to say, "What else you got?" Full disclosure, the horse did—seemingly reluctantly—walk and trot a little, but never did it canter. Bruce did though! Wyatt stepped in to put Bruce, and maybe the horse, out of his misery.

Wyatt looked at Bruce and asked him, "How long have you been competing with everything in your life to prove your worth?"

To which I leapt out of my chair and yelled, "It's TRUE!"

Bruce's belief that he had to constantly prove his worth had him constantly feeling like he wasn't good enough. Bruce is very handsome, an accomplished cardiologist, and such a warm, loving, kind, and non-judgmental person. And yet he never felt worthy.

The people, relationships, and circumstances of our lives, like the horse, will reflect back to us those self-limiting beliefs we are unknowingly acting on. This happens so we can become aware of those limiting beliefs. Once Bruce and I became conscious of those beliefs, we could choose to keep them or not. Thank goodness. My limiting belief that had me questioning Bruce frequently along with his limiting belief of never feeling worthy was a vicious circle that was very damaging to our relationship.

The horse therapy experience shows us how we can have beliefs that limit us – even ones we formed very early on in life. It can even happen while we're in the womb. In his book 'The Secrets of the Unborn Child', Thomas Verdy, MD, explains that the womb is the first world and establishes the child's expectations. He states that the unborn child absorbs the emotions and beliefs of the mother. Strongly. I could see this clearly with my own two children. I decided to have my first baby because I felt stuck in life. I was married and had a career but felt that something was missing. This baby was going to be the thing that fulfilled me and filled that void. This baby was going to save me from my unhappiness. This baby, Rachael, who is thirty-one years old now, has always believed that she is responsible for fixing other peoples' lives and making them happy. It has caused her much anxiety and angst all her life. I used to listen in shock when as a teenager she would tell me how stressed she was.

I would think and maybe even at times say, "You live in a beautiful home, play soccer very well, do well in school, have your own car, don't have to work…how can you be so stressed?" When I discovered that my feelings and emotions while pregnant with her had been absorbed by her, I finally understood where some, and maybe a lot, of her anxiety and stress came from. She had formed a belief that she was responsible for other people emotionally. She couldn't just play soccer for the fun of it. She unconsciously felt responsible for the coach, her teammates, and me because nothing made me happier in those days than watching her play soccer. It was the same with schoolwork. She felt the weight of the world on her shoulders to make others happy through her performance.

When Rachael was five months old, I got pregnant with my son. I did not want this baby. I had my baby, Rachael. I called my mom with what I said was 'the worst news'. I told her I was pregnant. Of course, my mom told me to pick myself up, everything was going to be fine, and this baby was going to be a good thing. I wholeheartedly did not agree. I did not want another baby. This baby, Nic, is now thirty years old and has never felt completely accepted, wanted, or valued. He's always had a lot of friends but has always felt left out in different ways. He would tell me stories like, "I was first in line at the bowling alley, and it was like the lady behind the counter didn't even see me. She just kept waiting on everyone else!" And, "My friends all got together and didn't even tell me." Nic is an extremely likable person. He's funny, outgoing, charismatic, and everyone tells me, "I love Nic." But even though I got over the shock of being pregnant again so soon and embraced and loved and wanted my baby Nic just as much as his sister, he carries the belief that he absorbed from me in the womb that he is not wanted or valued. To this day, it strongly influences his perspective and affects his relationships and career.

While I could clearly see the association of my emotions and feelings during pregnancy reflected in the subconscious beliefs of my children, I wanted to field test it on a friend before I introduced it in my life coaching sessions. One night, Rachael and I were out to dinner with (not their real names) our friends, Marcia, and her daughter, Darla. At one point, Rachael and Darla went to the restroom together, so I took the chance to ask Marcia what she had been feeling when she was pregnant with Darla. She said that while she was very excited about the new experience and adventure, she was also afraid of the unknown, as this was her first baby. Rachael and Darla returned to the table, having heard none of this conversation. Talk turned to Darla's career opportunity in New York City. I asked her how she felt about it. She answered, "I'm very excited about the new adventure and experience to live in NYC, but I'm also afraid of the unknown." Marcia and I looked at each other eyes wide with amazement.

Author Brent Baum shares this story about a boy named Justin: Justin has a left eye distorted by forty degrees. He 'remembers' his father shooting himself in his left eye – but that event had happened while Justin was in the womb.

The beliefs and experiences we absorbed while in the womb are strong. I would say they are the strongest subconscious beliefs we have. They seem to be almost cellular. Becoming aware of them does not make them instantly go away. But being aware of them does give us the opportunity of noticing when they are in the driver's seat of our lives.

We can then ask ourselves, "Am I really responsible for fixing other people's unhappiness?"

"Is it true that I am not wanted?"

"Do I have to be afraid of the unknown?"

Then there are the beliefs that we unknowingly form even as adults. Thirteen years ago, I went to a workshop about limiting beliefs. The workshop was being taught by Christel Nani, a registered nurse and medical intuitive. Christel can see the energy fields, known as chakras, emanating from our bodies. I was beyond excited. At this time, I had my bookstore and felt I was pretty in tune with how to navigate life in a spiritual/metaphysical way. I felt so sure of myself that the thought occurred to me that Christel might just ask me to help out in the workshop! (Not proud of this today.) Well, she did call on me. Actually, she called me out.

Christel came over and stood directly in front of me and asked, "What would you do if I said you were in my chair?"

I answered that I would try to figure out why she thought I was in her chair.

"So," she said, "you would just acquiesce? You would just roll over and let me have your chair?"

I said, "No. I would talk to you about why you think I'm in your chair."

She then got right in my face and yelled, "YOU'RE IN MY CHAIR! NOW what do you want to say to me?" she boomed.

This time I yelled back, "I'M NOT IN YOUR CHAIR!" except it came out more like, "$%*# YOU!" Actually, it came out exactly, "$%*# YOU!"

Christel then asked me to stand up. She told me that the energy of my second chakra, which has to do with a person's relationship with another person or thing, was completely black and stagnant. It is supposed to be orange and swirling. She told me that while she could see that, overall, I had a feisty blueprint, there were people in my life I let walk all over me. At first, I argued that that just wasn't true. She asked my friend who was with me if she noticed that in me. My friend said no. But Christel saw what she saw, and she urged me to look deeper. And then it hit me. It was my children. It was a hard realization. I immediately got a major headache. Christel could tell that I was shaken. She moved on to another participant. But at the break, she came up to me and asked how I was doing. She told me I had a belief that good moms have happy kids. She told me I was a doormat to my kids. And, although I had never realized it, I knew she was right. I divorced my kids' dad when they were very young. I felt that since I was responsible for their sadness—'bad Mom'—I was responsible for their happiness—'good Mom'. I had spent fourteen years jumping through any hoop they threw up just to make them happy. But they weren't, and neither was I. I

51

loved my kids deeply, but I taught them through my limiting belief to use me and exhaust me. I returned home from the workshop that Sunday determined to change my belief and, therefore, my energy and situation. My new belief became good moms love their kids and let them be responsible for their own happiness. My son, Nic, was a senior in high school at this time. Monday at lunchtime he came home for lunch, and I asked him what he'd like to eat. BLTs. Okay, I made BLTs. I set them down in front of him and he said, "They're burnt."

Shaking, and I mean literally shaking, I picked up the plate, went to the sink, and turned on the garbage disposal, fully prepared to dump them down the drain.

I said to him, "Make your own BLTs."

It was hard to do! He fell all over himself, apologizing and thanking me for making them. The energy had shifted because I had changed a belief I didn't even know I had. Two days later was my birthday. Nic went out on his own and bought me a birthday gift. He even wrapped it. And guess what it was…a doormat!

Limiting beliefs abound. The good news is that, regardless of where they come from, there is a way to bring them into our awareness so they can be looked at and resolved. Being under the influence of an unconscious limiting belief leaves us feeling like victims. Uncovering and rewriting those beliefs brings relief, renewed energy, and the wonderful feeling of empowerment. I developed a simple technique to help my clients become aware of their limiting beliefs. It's based on the premise that the situations and relationships in our lives will always mirror back to us the things we need to look at and resolve in ourselves.

It warrants repeating, "If you want to know what you believe, look at what you have in your life. Your life will always reflect your beliefs." Our beliefs become our perceptions and expectations. Notice what you notice in other people and situations. If it bugs you, or triggers any negative emotion in you, it's a reflection of a limiting belief you unconsciously hold.

Here's the technique:

I had my clients write down the names of three people in their lives. If they had a significant other, I asked them to include that person. The other two could be friends, co-workers, or other family members. Next to each person's name, I had them write what bugged them about that person. Even those we dearly love, and often especially those closest to us, have things about them that bother us. What's interesting and enlightening is that what bugs us in other people is actually a bug in us. There is a South African proverb that says the reason two antelope walk together is so that one can blow the dust from the other's eyes. We need each other to help blow the dust from our eyes and see what's actually behind those experiences we find unwelcome.

If it bugs you, it's about you. Some client stories:

Client #1

Her list of three people:

1. Her spouse
2. Her niece
3. A couple she and her husband were friends with

What bugged her:

1. Spouse: He used to put her on a pedestal but now pays way more attention to everyone else.
2. Niece: Doesn't answer client's phone calls or texts for days or weeks, even though said niece is never without her phone.
3. Friends: Client is completely ignored when she and her husband go out with these friends. No one pays any attention to her even when she tries to join the conversation.

While you might be inclined to place blame on the husband, niece, and friends, remember that if it bugs you, it's about you. Blame is insane. If what is showing up in our lives is coming from a belief we are not aware of, how can we blame the people in our lives who are merely reflecting that belief back to us?

Looking at what bugged my client about each person, a common theme presents itself. A theme of being ignored, not being included, and not being important. Following Rule #1 (follow the emotion), I asked my client—and this is key—if she had ever felt this way before in her life. "All my life," was her answer. Most limiting beliefs have been around, as we've seen, since birth or early childhood. Feelings generated by our interactions with others as adults will feel very familiar. This client had been the fourth of four children and felt that she had never really been wanted by her mom. Whether this was actually true or not doesn't matter. (Remember, when we are in a theta brain wave, we don't interpret things logically.) Her perception that she was not wanted is what mattered. Because of this perception, my client formed an unconscious belief of 'I don't matter'. This belief was being reflected back to her in her current relationships. Co-workers weren't on her list of three, but this client often shared the deep hurt she felt by being shunned by her co-workers. The belief she formed as a young girl that she didn't matter was now informing most of the relationships in her life. Have you ever heard the expression that you teach people how to treat you? It's like when I was 'teaching' my children to treat me like a doormat. They could feel my energy and it was saying, "I owe you."

This client's energy was saying, "Treat me like I don't matter, because I don't." She wasn't aware of this. All she knew was that she felt really, really sad and bad because of how she was being treated. She felt like a victim. There are few things more disempowering than feeling like a victim. Once we were able to bring this belief into her awareness, she could look at it and decide consciously if she still believed it. Did she, at fifty-plus years old, believe she didn't matter? No! It was time to rewrite that limiting belief into a self-affirming belief. Christel Nani taught me to start the rewrite of a limiting belief with the phrase, "It's reasonable to believe _____." Together, this client and I composed some options: "It's reasonable to believe I matter." "It's reasonable to believe all people matter." "It's reasonable to believe I have value." But it wasn't until we came up with 'It's reasonable to believe everyone has a unique way of mattering and I love my uniqueness' that she felt her energy shift. It takes some playing with it to get the rewrite to deeply resonate, but it is imperative that it does, and deeply. The rewrite must touch you all the way down to your toes and back. Otherwise, it's just words, your energy doesn't change, and the energy of the limiting belief remains and nothing in your life changes. It was a beautiful thing to see this client own her worth and become empowered. It changed her life. No longer was she giving the value of herself over to everyone else in her life and constantly, unconsciously, asking them to validate her. She was no longer a victim. She glowed. And once she changed her energy, the people in her life started treating her differently. Like she matters!

Client #2

Her list of three people:

1. Her spouse
2. A co-worker
3. A friend

What bugged her:

1. Spouse: Had no drive or motivation. Would rather drink beer.
2. Co-worker: Did not want to get ahead in her career. Lazy.
3. Friend: Afraid to speak up for herself.

The common theme here is holding oneself back. This client had a fear of speaking up for her own needs, and this fear was preventing her from moving forward in her life. Interestingly, not only were the relationships in her life reflecting this back to her but so was her body. She had a severe spine problem – no backbone, not sticking up for herself. The spine problem led to foot drop, which made it hard for her to walk – forward motion.

This client left life coaching before we could name her actual belief and rewrite it, but if she had continued, we would have come up with some flavor of 'I'm not worthy' because all limiting beliefs are about self-worth. It might have been something like 'I'm not worth the trouble'. "Who am I to ask for what I need and want?" "It's not okay to let the real me be seen."

You may be wondering why I would include a client who didn't stay with life coaching long enough to figure out her major limiting belief. Let me first say that this particular 'client' was actually an informal consult I did as a favor to a friend. I don't think she was as interested in becoming aware of her limiting beliefs as her friend wanted her to be. But what I'm going to share with you next makes her case interesting on yet another level.

The very first exercise I would do with my clients was what I called the Vision. It is a way to access the subconscious mind and show the client just how in the know our subconscious minds are. In the Vision process, the client closes their eyes and I ask them to visualize a field of sand. Next, I ask them to add a cube to that vision. Unbeknownst to the client, the cube represents the clients' sense of themselves. Their identity, value, how they see themselves in life. Every cube from each client was different. I never got the same description of a cube twice, except for two Rubik's cubes. This wasn't surprising, however, as both of those clients were engineers and it made total sense that they would come up with a Rubik's cube to represent their sense of themselves. One client described her cube as a pallet of sorts, and in life, she was a doer and loved being instrumental in getting things done. I bring this up to share with you what Client #2's cube was. It was an ice cube almost completely buried in the sand. Only the very top was able to be seen. Our limiting beliefs live in our subconscious mind. And since our subconscious mind is so dominant, what's in our subconscious is majorly influencing our perceptions and expectations.

Unfortunately, we did not get to rewrite this client's limiting belief into a self-affirming belief. But this is a good place to point out that 99% of the time, it does not work to simply say the opposite of the limiting belief. If this client's limiting belief was 'It's not okay for the real me to be seen', rewriting it to 'It's okay for the real me to be seen', most likely isn't going to deeply resonate. Here are a couple of rewrite options to help the reader: "No one knows better than me what would make me happy and fulfilled." "Everyone has the right to pursue their own happiness." "Pursuing my wants and desires does not stop anyone else from pursuing theirs."

Since I brought up in this client's example how subconscious limiting beliefs can be reflected through our bodies, I'd like to share another story that further illuminates this phenomenon. I was not a life coach at this time, but I did have my bookstore and had by this time read many of the books I would later use to develop my life coaching process. The very first customer that came into my store was a man I'll call Felix. Felix would come in about once a week to browse the books and chat with me. One night, he told me he wouldn't be coming in the following Friday because he had rehearsal. Felix played in the local symphony orchestra as a professional. The following Friday night was a cold, blizzardy one, and no one was venturing into the bookstore. Except

Felix. I was surprised to see him as he had said he wouldn't be coming and because the weather was so bad. When I asked him why he wasn't at rehearsal, he told me that he had a kidney stone and wasn't feeling well. I asked him if he'd like to look into what this kidney stone might be trying to tell him about his life. He agreed, and we pulled Louise Hays's book You Can Heal Your Life off the shelf. The book said that a kidney stone indicates 'lumps of unresolved anger'. I questioned Felix about being angry. He answered, "You bet I am! The orchestra is cutting back our salaries to the point that I may have to move out of my house. I'm sick and tired of them not valuing us." Rule #1: Follow the emotion.

'Felix, have you ever felt not valued before in your life?' I asked.

He answered, "All my life."

He shared that whenever he auditioned for a spot in a musical ensemble, from the time he was just starting out as a child, he had to audition behind a screen. He felt that if the judges actually saw him, they wouldn't value his abilities. I inquired as to whether he was still interested in giving the opinion of his value/worth over to others, rather than giving that opinion to himself. "Absolutely not!" was his response. I didn't see Felix for four to five months after that night. When I did see him, I was amazed. He had lost weight, lost the anger, and was vibrant and full of enthusiasm. He had started playing golf and had also found the love of his life. I don't know if you play golf or not, but playing golf is like auditioning without a curtain – every swing. All eyes are on you. He was truly a changed man all because he made the choice to let his worth and value come from inside himself.

Client #3

Her list of three:

1. Her boss
2. Her spouse
3. Her dad

What bugged her:

1. Boss: None of her ideas were ever good enough.
2. Husband: Never praised her even if she made a terrific meal.
3. Dad: She had to live up to his extremely high expectations of her.

The common theme here is one of outside approval for worthiness. This client gave the value of her ideas, her offerings, her performances, and herself over to others instead of getting it from herself. She resonated deeply with this. I then invoked Rule #1: "Have you ever felt this way before in your life?" At this point, she shared that as a young girl she was quite good at golf. Golf became a big part of her identity and her father put major pressure on her regarding it. At one point, he even told her that if she didn't start winning tournaments, he would kill himself. This client formed a strong belief that external validation of her abilities was what mattered. She sought this validation in everything she did. She had stopped doing things for the pleasure of doing them. Everything had to be a performance that she conquered in order to get a good grade from others. Her subconscious self-limiting belief: My worth belongs to the opinion of others. We were able to rewrite this to the self-affirming belief: Doing things for the joy they bring is all the validation I need.

If you find yourself feeling like a victim, like you want to blame another person or situation for what's happening in your emotional and physical life, it more than likely is coming from a belief you don't know you have. When you feel affronted or attacked in any way, take the arrow out of your heart and examine it. Forget who shot it 'at you'. How does it make you feel? If you've felt that way often in your life, look for the limiting belief behind that feeling. Blame is insane because it's your limiting belief that is driving the perception and negative feeling you experience. The people and situations in your life are simply mirroring that belief back to you.

The best way to keep a prisoner a prisoner is to never let them know they are a prisoner. Most of us have been prisoners of our limiting beliefs because we didn't know we had them. In her book 'You Are a Badass', Jen Sincero says that limiting beliefs are like having one foot on the gas and the other one on the brake. It's time we set ourselves free. Fortunately for us, our souls want to be released from the bondage of beliefs that hold us back, and so life will show us what we believe through what bugs us about the relationships, people, and situations we experience. Those beliefs that offered us acceptance and security while we were young are being shown to us so we can move beyond them and be free. Free to accept, love, and embrace our uniqueness, passions, desires, preferences, and, therefore, our worth. Oh, and by the way, the whispers become shouts. The 'what bugs yous' in your life won't go away if you ignore them or try to move away from them. You take yourself wherever you go, and they are a part of you. The negative influences they exert will just get bigger and stronger. Patterns point to their purpose. Crypto-analysts look for patterns to break codes and find the real meaning behind what is being presented. If you recognize a pattern of a feeling in your life – being misunderstood, feeling unimportant, always taken advantage of, that you're never good enough, feeling responsible for other people's happiness; the list goes on and on – look for a limiting belief that is behind that pattern. Break the code.

Become Yourself

- Do the next joyful thing.
    - You know what you want by what you don't want.
    - What's the essence behind the form?
    - Does it raise my vibrations?

- Become aware of and rewrite self-limiting beliefs.
    - If it bugs you, it's about you.
    - Blame is insane.
    - Notice what you notice.
    - Who built your box and why are you still in it?
    - Whispers become shouts.
    - Patterns point to their purpose.
    - If you want to know what you believe, look at what you have in your life. Your life always reflects your beliefs.

```
┌─────────────────────────────────────────────────────────┐
│                    PERMISSION SLIP                        │
│                                                           │
│   I give myself permission to                             │
│                                                           │
│   _____│
│   _____│
└─────────────────────────────────────────────────────────┘
```

Chapter 4
Follow the Grain in
Your Own Wood

A good life is one where you develop your strengths, realize
your potential, and become what it is in your nature to
become.

— Aristotle

I gotta be me.

— Sammy Davis Jr.

Be what you is cuz if you ain't what you is you is what you
ain't.

— found on a tombstone in Texas

HAVE YOU EVER SAID, "So and so is a natural
_____?" A natural public speaker, hostess,
entertainer, mother, businessperson? Or "So and so is a born
_____?" Born teacher, storyteller, or explorer? We
all have our own natural and unique characteristics and bents.
Our grain in our own wood. These are the energies we were
born with and have our entire lives. They strongly contribute

to our personalities. They dictate what we prefer and enjoy and what we don't prefer and enjoy. They provide us with the pathway that will bring us the most satisfaction and nourishment in life. And when viewed as a whole, they are a blueprint for our purpose, or plan, for this life, and how to fully enjoy it.

However, just because these energies are innate in us does not mean we automatically embrace them or are even consciously aware of them. Thanks to our original way of seeking happiness, through acceptance, we learned to ignore or deny some or most of our natural personalities. We didn't want to be different or weird. We judged ourselves and in the process made ourselves not only not ourselves, but unhappy and dissatisfied as well. It has been said that self-judgment is the number one cause of unhappiness in the world.

Discovering your unique, natural abilities is like getting to know yourself at a soul level. Embracing them is saying 'yes' to your authentic self. Living within them is like wearing the clothes you feel most comfortable in.

In his book 'Living with the Monks', Jesse Itzler shares that the greatest challenge in life is discovering who you are, and the second greatest is being happy with what you find. As I said earlier, on my journey to becoming myself, I would read things like the answers are all inside of you, and a good guru will always point you back to yourself. I believed this was wise and good advice. The psychic had done just that by asking me to get in touch with what made me joyful – and do it. What is necessary is that your life works for you. What makes me joyful and fulfilled is not necessarily, or even likely, to be what makes you joyful and fulfilled. What makes each of us empowered is being authentic. But authentic to what? Authentic to the natural energies and qualities we were born with. What's a sundial in the shade?

Here again, what we did as children for play can give us a big clue as to what some of those natural proclivities are. Did you love playing school and being the student? Did you love assembling models? Were you fascinated by how things worked? Were you always the leader? I have a nephew who as a toddler was obsessed with flushing toilets. He was on a mission to find the best flushing toilet out there. He would go into a friend or relative's home and ask if he could flush all of their toilets. He is now in engineering school. (And, by the way, he surmised that TOTO has the best flushing toilets available). Remembering what interested us as children is a good way to find connections to our natural energies. It's a good start. But to get the broadest and most comprehensive awareness of just what those natural inclinations are, we need to look at our archetypes, astrology, and ancestry.

I'd be willing to bet that most people have never heard of archetypes. And I'd also be willing to bet that most of us have heard of astrology. Ancestry, that we inherit characteristics of ourselves, is widely accepted. As far as archetypes go, I think, like myself and my clients, you'll find the discovery of your archetypes fun and empowering. I realize the mixed opinions about astrology and its relevance or even validity. Religious beliefs concerning astrology aside, my clients and I found it very helpful in identifying energies they were born with.

ARCHETYPES

The word 'archetype' is derived from the Greek roots 'archein' and 'typos'. 'Archein' meaning 'first, to begin or to rule' and 'typos' meaning 'pattern or model'. Archetypes are molds or models of archaic energy that can still be related to by everyone worldwide. As an example, 'detective' is an archetype, and detective energy is an archetypal energy that people can resonate with. A person with keen observation skills, who is good at solving puzzles and is solution-oriented, fits the mold or model of a detective. This person has a detective archetype. They have detective energy. It doesn't mean that the person is working as a detective for their career. It means the person has the qualities of a detective. This energy comes naturally to them.

Naming energies as archetypes is not new. The first mention of archetypes dates back to the fifth century BCE, during the times of Plato. More recently, Carl Jung understood archetypes as 'universal, archaic patterns and images that derive from the collective unconscious and are the psychic counterpart of instinct'. [7] I was introduced to archetypes by modern-day medical intuitive Carolyn Myss, through her book Sacred Contracts. Carolyn Myss is said to have brought the understanding and use of archetypes into the twenty-first century. In the book, she shares how, while tuning into the energy of her clients, she noticed an 'organizing principle' to these energies. The energy was organized into different archetypes or molds. She deduced that we each have roughly eight archetypes that are unique to us. It's in discovering these archetypes that we can become acquainted with our authentic selves energetically.

What are archetypes? Natural energies we possess.

Who has archetypes? Everyone.

When are our archetypes active? Always.

---

[7] Wikipedia.

Where do archetypes live? In the collective unconscious.

How do they influence us? Through our intuition.

Why do we have them? To help us realize our life plans and contracts for happiness and fulfillment.

Archetypes are one key to the real us, to our authentic selves. They speak to our essence. Archetypes in their purest form point us to our joy.

Archetypal references abound in everyday language. In my poker group, I became known as the 'queen' because I was willing to make decisive rulings readily. Some of the more common archetypal references are hero, princess, God/god, fool, vampire, addict, athlete, angel, Don Juan, engineer – you get the picture.

In life coaching, I referred to the Archetype, Astrology, and Ancestry (AAA) sessions as the 'Mother May I?' sessions. Did you play that game growing up? In the version I played, one friend would be the 'mother' and stand on the front porch. The rest of us, playing the 'children', would stand at the far end of the sidewalk and wait to be commanded by the mother to 'take five giant steps forward' or 'take three baby steps backwards'. The commands were completely at the whim of the mother. We children had to ask, "Mother, may I?" before carrying out the command. Failing to ask this meant you got sent all the way back to the starting point. Oh, and the mother could also simply deny your request of, "Mother, may I?" The mother had all the control. I called the AAA sessions the 'Mother May I?' sessions because I wanted my clients to see the lunacy of asking someone else permission for their forward movement in life. I wanted them to start giving themselves permission by listening to their own internal guidance. This internal guidance/preference, born out of our AAA energies, comes to us, like Jung said, through our instincts and intuition. I would always tell my mom that I was born to be a mother. I just felt it. We often ignore it, for reasons we've already discussed. We got trained to seek outside ourselves for permission or support in following our hunches. And, all too often, we don't get that support because others would rather have us do what works for them rather than what makes us feel good. Mother, may I? No. You may not. What?

I had a client who was extremely successful in her career. She traveled a lot for said career and stayed many nights in hotels. While on the road, every night after work, her co-workers wanted her to go out with them for dinner and drinks. And every night, all she wanted to do was go back to her hotel room and be alone. She berated herself for this desire, thinking that she must be odd and have something wrong with her. She knew going out after work did not raise her vibrations, but she judged herself for not having the same desires as her colleagues. When we identified her eight unique archetypes, we discovered that she had a 'hermit' archetype. Hermits need time alone every day to rejuvenate. This discovery was amazingly empowering to my client. She was immensely relieved. Instantly, she was able to love and embrace that part of herself. No more asking others if she should want to be alone as part of her daily routine. She now knew and owned that need as part of her natural make-up and to deny it would not be in her own best interest. This client was finally able to permit herself to follow her intuition. For the first time in her career, she could act on what did raise her vibrations with zero guilt or self-judgment.

When the 'rebel' showed up as one of my eight unique-to-me archetypes, I was not surprised. I love to make to-do lists but would often look at them afterward and think, *Who are you to tell me what to do?* I was rebelling against my own list! Looking over my life, I could clearly see how rebel energy was always a part of it. Often, I would shoot myself in the foot with it, sabotaging even my own intentions. The rebel, however, is someone who is willing and ready to move beyond what has always been. Someone who does not merely accept the status quo. Rebels are able to break old tribal patterns and beliefs. I strongly resonated with these rebel attributes and feel they were instrumental in my quest to find the meaning of life and the meaning of my life, outside of the religious beliefs I had been taught. If you've ever been called the black sheep of your family, you could very well have a rebel archetype. I embrace my rebel energy for the courage it gives me to forge my own path. And I also recognize when it wants to sabotage my to-do list. I realize that I will always tend to bring rebel energy to my life's situations because it is a part of my natural personality and always will be. Becoming aware of it allows me to decide when it's helpful or hindering.

The eight archetypes that are unique for each of us are like eight pieces of a puzzle that, when put together, give us the knowledge of why we prefer what we do in life. I would tell my clients, "You can choose to align with what makes you feel good, drives you, and brings meaning to your life, but you can't choose what makes you feel good, drives you, and brings meaning to your life." Allow me to clarify that. Of course, you can choose what to do in your life. But if you make those choices outside of your natural traits, talents, and personality, your journey will require more effort and, ultimately, be less satisfying. Your archetypes, astrology, and ancestry (with a caveat regarding ancestry that we will go into later in this chapter) are like the black squares in a crossword puzzle. They create a framework. They aren't negotiable. They allow you to fill in the white squares, which represent how you choose to express and live your natural energies. For example, with a 'teacher' archetype I could have chosen to become a schoolteacher to express that part of myself. I didn't. Instead, my teacher energy came through me, among other ways, as a mom, bookstore owner, life coach, and now as a writer. There are countless ways to express our archetypal energies, but we each don't have countless archetypes. Not major ones, anyway. Sharing with my clients the eight unique-to-them archetypes we together revealed, I would refer to them as their 'meat and potatoes' archetypes, the main dish. Everyone also had several archetypal influences that I called 'spices'. But the important point is to know when something resonates with you or not and to express the things that do somehow in your life.

I think it's also important to clarify that it's not selfish, in the negative connotation of 'being selfish' to become aware of what natural energies you have and make the choice to align with them. It's been said, and I agree, that most humans have a deep desire to know their purpose because, ultimately, the human is a being of service, and to know one's purpose is to know one's path of service. How you matter is by what matters to you. I like to use a simple analogy to bring this point home. Let's say your child's class is having a Valentine's Day party and you are asked to bake cookies. You loathe baking cookies. It's just not you. You could agree to make those cookies, against every fiber in your being, and then spend the next week dreading the cookies, procrastinating shopping for the ingredients, finally throwing together the batch and, most likely, burning at least some of them. Making cookies just is not in your wheelhouse. But creating fun is! You could decline to bake cookies but offer to create new and fun games for the kids to play at the party. The energy drain you felt upon being asked to bake cookies suddenly becomes an exhilarating project. You look forward to bringing to fruition the ideas that are already starting to pop into your thoughts. You spend satisfying time in the craft store gathering the supplies needed. Your passion is infectious as you play the games with the students and see the fun they're having, too. When we agree to do something outside of our authentic energies, even something as seemingly small as baking cookies, it is a big drain on our overall energy. In fact, that's one way to know if you're being authentic or not. If you're feeling drained by the things you agree to do in your life, be aware that you are acting outside of your natural energies and talents. Vice versa: If you're acting within your archetypal energies, the action and time you put into whatever you're doing will feel effortless.

In their book 'The Spirituality of Imperfection', authors Emest Kurtz and Katherine Ketcham say that the rule of thumb in the animal kingdom is 'eat or be eaten'. In the human kingdom, it is 'define or be defined'. Who is defining you? Who built your box? Within whose ideas of what you should be doing are you being boxed? A very nice side effect, if you will, of knowing and embracing your true nature is the clear boundaries this authentic way of living provides. "Want to go to dinner and get drinks?" "No, thank you, but I look forward to seeing everyone in the morning." "Can you bake cookies?" "Baking cookies just isn't me. How can I help in other ways?" Being authentic makes our yes a yes, as well as our no a no. Without apologies. Boundaries are actually very freeing.

While being true to our nature and preferences gives us clear boundaries, we still have to be willing to use those boundaries. Here is where vulnerability comes in. Not everyone is going to understand or appreciate our boundaries. In addition to rebel and teacher, in my eight archetypes I also have 'philosopher', 'celibate', and 'hermit' archetypes. Celibate can refer to sexual celibacy, but in my case, it refers to my desire to be away from distractions in order to focus and create. Philosophers, hermits, and celibates like their 'me time'. I need a lot of 'me time'. I don't like crowds or being part of a group. I have developed strong boundaries around these energies and rarely accept an invitation to join group activities. I'm not a lady who lunches. Over the years, my friends and family have accepted these traits in me. For those who don't know me well, however, I can be taken as, for lack of a better term, 'stuck-up'. I lived in Kansas for four years, and while there I worked one night a week as an RN at the Kansas City Heart Institute. Combining not being there very often and therefore not getting that close with my co-workers, with my natural tendencies to be alone, I would spend my nights outside my patients' rooms, charting, keeping a close watch on them, and assisting my fellow nurses when they asked me for help. At my yearly review, my head nurse told me that my colleagues complained that I was stuck-up. Her answer to them was that was just my 'East Coast mentality'. I'm from Ohio. So not East Coast. Did it bother me? I have to admit, it did a little. But it was just me being me. Ultimately, I was good with that.

Based on the pioneering (an archetypal word) work of both Carolyn Myss and Christel Nani, I developed an Archetype Assessment Tool. Through this two-step questionnaire, my clients and I were able to bring to light their eight unique-to-them archetypal energies, giving them this piece of their very own blueprint for their happiness and personal purpose. When I was first starting out on my quest to find my personal purpose, I believed I had a specific, almost predestined purpose for my time here on earth. Now my understanding is that my purpose is born out of the energies I was born with, and that purpose is to embrace those qualities and create ways to express them that content and fulfil me.

Knowing our archetypes is empowering. I gave my clients archetype cards. Each archetype had its own card on which the energy of that archetype is displayed artistically. One client actually had her cards framed and hung them in her home. They represented her in a way that she had never known before and meant so very much to her. Her archetypes are 'knight', 'servant', 'mother', 'pioneer', 'engineer', 'seeker', 'teacher' and 'student'. I share these with you not only because I find them interesting and intriguing but because when we get to the astrology part of this chapter, we'll compare her archetypal and astrological energies to show how they complement and support each other.

This discussion on archetypes barely scratches the surface of their scope and usefulness. It's only my intention to make you aware that you have them and that getting to know them is an essential part of becoming yourself. Sadly, I can't provide you with the Archetype Assessment Tool, as it was a collaborative process between my clients and me, and so requires that I be involved. I recommend that you read Sacred Contracts by Carolyn Myss. It is an excellent and informative book that guides you through the revelation of your eight unique-to-you archetypes...and much, much more.

ASTROLOGY

The word astrology is a loaded one. It can conjure up anything from daily horoscopes to the real and exciting study of the celestial bodies and their electromagnetic influence on the world. Some people believe in it, some don't. In his book 'When the Impossible Happens', psychiatrist Stanislov Grof, one of the founders of the field of transpersonal psychology, shares that he did not believe in the influences of astrology. But after over fifty years of consciousness research, Grof made this statement: "One of the greatest surprises I have experienced over the fifty years that I have been involved in consciousness research was the discovery of the predictive power of astrology and cosmobiological forces." He isn't alone. Hippocrates said, "A physician who has no knowledge of astrology has no right to call himself a physician." The framers of our Constitution were men who strongly believed that the stars and fate were intertwined.[8] These men paid close attention to the layout of the heavens as they structured the new world. The cornerstones of the Federal Triangle—the Capitol, the White House, and the Washington Monument—were laid in different years but were all carefully timed to occur under the exact same astrological condition known as

---

[8] "The DaVinci Code" by Dan Brown.

Caput Draconius in Virgo. Our good friend Carl Jung perceived astrology to be the greatest tool of psychological analysis known to man. Isaac Newton and Albert Einstein also considered that astrological insights offer us a profound understanding of human personality. Edgar Cayce, the man known as the sleeping prophet, found that within most of his 14,000 readings there were references to specific astrological influences bearing on the lives of his clients. He stated, "When studied right it is very, very, very worthwhile to study the influence of the planets on our lives." The Jewish phrase 'Mazel Tov', which is an expression of congratulations or wishing someone good luck, translates as "May a benevolent astrological constellation shine upon you."

Astrology is the world's oldest science. It is an extensive field of study and one that is way too complex for me to wrap my head around. But, when I read, "True astrology is the art of identifying a person's uniqueness,"[9] that got my interest. At this time, I was developing my life coaching process and didn't want to discount anything that could assist me and my clients to discover more of their authentic selves. I wasn't interested in the predictive power of astrology, such as a horoscope for the future, but more about how the energy of the celestial arrangement at the time of our birth influences our makeup. And if minds much more evolved than mine believed in it, who was I to disregard it?

How can the heavens influence our personalities and uniqueness? I view it like smartphones that can sync up to each other simply by being in close proximity. The electromagnetic energy emitted by the planets, stars, and

---

[9] "Crossing the Bridge to the Future" by Mark Borax.

other celestial bodies at the time of our birth synced up with our own electromagnetic energy. This is how I understand it, but really the proof is in the pudding. Would my clients reverberate with the astrological information we uncovered for them or not?

I was led to two main sources for this information. One is The Secret Language of Destiny: A Personology Guide to Finding Your Life Purpose by Gary Goldschneider and Joost Effers. I love that subtitle, A Personology Guide to Finding Your Life Purpose. The second source is Sacred Symbols of the Ancients by Edith L. Randall and Florence Evelyn Campbell. Both resources became invaluable as, one by one, each client was awed, amazed, and astonished at the resonance they felt with the material.

Knowing our natural archetypal and astrological characteristics gives us an even more detailed blueprint, or framework, for knowing how to express ourselves in ways that will give us meaning and happiness. It also gives us permission to be ourselves.

Perhaps the best way to present the impact of astrological information on my clients is to share a client's story.

We'll call her Framer. Framer is the client who framed her archetype cards. Framer has three server archetypes – knight-servant-mother. She is a natural at serving, so said her archetypes. And so did her astrology. Her astrology informed us that hers is a path of making the world a better place, that she is service-oriented and receptive by nature. It said she would have many 'children' to make sacrifices for and that she has a natural inclination to help and nurture others. Framer also has four innovative archetypes – pioneer-seeker-student-engineer. Her astrology told us that she has a strong and natural belief that anything is possible. It said she has a fondness for traveling and moving as she has a thirst for adventure that keeps her searching for what lies ahead. Her astrology revealed she loves to ponder the big questions of life. Rounding out Framer's eight unique archetypes was that of teacher. This archetypal energy was complemented by her astrology, telling us she is a natural leader on a path of harvesting the wheat from the chaff and giving her wisdom to the world. It said she has abundant mental gifts to assist her in this.

Before knowing anything about these archetypal and astrological energies, Framer's answer to one of my initial interview questions of 'What is the purpose of life?' was 'I want to make a difference whether for me or for a hundred people'. Pretty impressive! She was in tune with her natural energies. But she was also the client who answered in response to my question of 'How in charge of your life do you feel?' with 'Negative 150%! I don't feel in charge of my life at all'.

How can a person who knows what she wants out of life feel so powerless? Self-limiting beliefs. As stated in the previous chapter, they are the biggest contributor to our overall vibration, and they run the show until we uncover them and rewrite them. Framer's major limiting belief was, "I need to do what others want me to do in order to belong." Framer had the natural personality and character traits to nurture people, herself, and ideas. But up until this point in her life, she had used these energies for the will of others, for what others wanted to take from her. Thankfully, getting the archetypal and astrological validation of her gifts—gifts she could use to live her purpose—was so empowering to Framer that she realized it was time to stop needing to belong in the eyes of others and to start belonging to her own desires and goals. By the end of our time together, Framer felt 'eighty percent' more in charge of her life.

Whether you believe in archetypes and astrology or not, believe in yourself. Listen to your gut. You really do know when something interests you or it doesn't. Accepting and embracing what thrills and fulfils you is you, maybe for the first time, becoming aware of you. Having the willingness to be vulnerable and make the decisions that align with those things is you becoming yourself.

ANCESTRY

As I write this, my son is seeking proof. Proof that he is a 'Viking'. Why? Because his doctor told him he needed to lose weight. While Nic agrees he could stand to lose a few pounds, he truly believes that it is his Viking ancestry at play here. He is 'overweight' only because his Viking bones, muscles, and general build make him weigh more than well, you know, non-Vikings.

Many people are interested in knowing their genetic ancestry. Most are not looking for justification for being bigger than their doctor thinks they should be. (In my son's defense, he did stand in the middle of the kitchen when he was 18 months old and clench his fists, flex his arms in front of his body, and yell at the top of his lungs, "AAAARRRGGGGHHH!" He might have a case.) There's a line in Sue Monk Kidd's book The Invention of Wings that says, "If you don't know where you're going, you should know where you came from." Knowing where we came from can be another piece to the puzzle of who we naturally are.

Author Dani Shapiro thought she knew where she came from. But at age fifty-four she found out through DNA testing that the father who had loved her, raised her, and steeped her deeply into his Orthodox Jewish faith and ancestral family was not her biological father. A sperm donor was. In her book 'Inheritance', Dani Shapiro asks the question, "What do we inherit, and how, and why?" A good book, and a good question. Ms. Shapiro was asking herself these very things as she, in shock and grief, tried to make sense of who she really was. Now. Was she related to the scores of Jewish, many famous, ancestors that she had grown up to respect, love, and cherish on her father's side of the family? Is it only inheritable if it's genetic? What of cultural beliefs, cultural traditions, and culture itself? Ms. Shapiro shares that all her life she sensed she really didn't belong in her family. She looked different. Many, many people throughout her life told her that she couldn't be Jewish. She just didn't look Jewish. In this book, she writes, "My father and I had shared a history, a culture, a landscape, a home, a language (Hebrew), an entire world. Our bond was real and unbreakable. But I also knew in the starkest terms, what had been missing: mutual recognition. I hadn't come from him. I had never once looked into his face and seen my own." What is it about ancestral heredity that connects us to who we are as individuals? I think it's that at our very core of cores, we crave to belong. Feeling like a misfit in her family as a little girl, Dani tells of wandering the neighborhood streets just before dark, seeing the lit-up houses with families gathered inside, and wishing she belonged to one of them. Now, here again, at age fifty-four, she was desperately wondering how she belonged. Through love, guidance, time, and the support of friends and family, Dani Shapiro was able to embrace all three contributors to her inheritance: her mother and father and her biological father (whom she got to meet and develop a relationship with). Dani brings up a Hebrew phrase in her book – L'dor Vador. It means 'from generation to generation'. What gets inherited, how, and why? Perhaps it's genes, culture, and love; three ways to belong.

My maternal grandmother's maiden name was Jung. Is it a coincidence that I have a passion for steeping myself in what's underneath the surface of life and consciousness? Perhaps not, perhaps so. Genetics research through 23&me tells me I have a substantial Irish heritage. Is this why my absolute favorite food is potatoes? Maybe...My mother-in-law was hurt and offended that I didn't call to chat with her very often. (Okay never.) When I explained that I rarely spoke with my own mom on the phone—it's just not appealing to either of us—she understood better that it wasn't about her.

We are each, at least partially, a product of all the ancestors who came before us, both genetically and culturally. By 'culture', I mean the cultures of our ancestral countries, our communities, society, and also the culture of the family we grew up in. My clients and I did not explore their specific ancestries, but we included ancestral influence because it is a part of who you are. My intention was to get them to recognize a trait in themselves, consider that it could be ancestral, and choose to embrace those traits with which they resonated. But what about those traits with which they did not resonate? Were they destined to live out their genetics or cultural biases and beliefs?

In the late 1980s, scientists undertook the Human Genome Project. Its purpose was to catalog all the genes humans possess. Contemporary thought believed they would find at least 120,000 different genes in the human body. Clearly, our abilities to think, decide, learn, remember, create, etc. would require a lot of genes. Imagine their shock and surprise when they discovered the human genome contained fewer than 25,000 different genes. Humans had only 1,500 more genes than the microscopic, spineless, thousand-celled Caenorhabditis worm. Only 9,000 more than fruit flies. And about the same as mice. Humans have over fifty trillion cells, yet only 25,000 genes.[10] The conclusion was that 'something' above the genes was telling these 25,000 genes how to combine to create the abilities and characteristics of a human. They called this 'something' epigenetic control. According to cell biologist Bruce Lipton, PhD, that something is our emotions, thoughts, and attitudes. Stress causes those genes to combine to make the stress hormone cortisol. Bliss calls the genes to combine to create endorphins. Our emotions, thoughts, and attitudes determine what our genes express! Data shows that emotions determine the actual patterning of DNA in the body.[11]

If this sounds a little far out to you, consider persons with Dissociative Identity Disorder (DID, formerly known as Multiple Personality Disorder). In the same body—same genes—one personality can have a severe allergy to orange juice, causing water-filled welts to form on their body, while the other personalities do not. One personality can be drunk and rely on one of the other sober personalities to drive her home. One can be right-handed while all others are left-handed. Prescription eyeglasses may be absolutely necessary

---

[10] "The Biology of Belief" by Bruce Lipton, PhD.
[11] "Walking Between the Worlds" by Gregg Baden.

to one personality and the others have 20/20 vision. According to Frank Putnam, MD, a psychologist who did research at the National Institute for Mental Health on persons with DID, some personalities could have signs of pregnancy, tumors, and cysts, while the others had none of these signs.[12]

Family history can be an important risk factor in certain disease processes, and I would be remiss (and pooh-poohed by my doctor husband) to suggest that it can be disregarded or ignored. I say factor it in but don't marry it. Things may have been set in motion by our ancestral DNA, but they aren't set in stone.

In his book 'Change Your Genes, Change Your Life', Dr. Kenneth Pelletier talks about a study done on identical twins at Johns Hopkins University. The study found that one twin could develop Parkinson's disease while the other twin showed only a five-percent chance of getting it. They found that in twins, coronary heart disease occurred only fifty percent of the time in both twins, which is the same as random chance. And, in the case of most cancers, the chance of both twins getting the cancer was less than fifty percent. In 2012, Dr. Bert Vogelstein, also of Johns Hopkins University, announced the results of a genetic study done on thousands of identical twins. He stated that disease cannot be predicted by genes alone other than in exceptional cases.

Culturally speaking, the preacher of a church I once attended told the story of a woman who always cut the back part of a roast off before putting it in the pan and oven. When asked why she did this, she said it was because her mom always did. Curious, she asked her mom why it was that she

---

[12] National Alliance on Mental Illness.

always cut off the back portion of a roast. Her mom answered that her roasting pan was too small to fit the whole roast.

Just like genetic DNA, cultural, societal, and family dynamic 'DNA' is passed down, as well. It's up to us to examine what has been passed on to us and recognize when we're doing something only because that's the way it's always been done. Maintaining beliefs and practices we truly embrace and enjoy and letting go of those things we don't resonate with is within our power.

Once we're born, our archetypes, astrology, and our ancestry are ours. The question is, what are we going to do with what we have? In the case of archetypes and astrology, will we look for and embrace our natural and authentic desires and preferences? In the case of ancestry, will we choose thoughts, emotions, and attitudes that help our genes work for us rather than against us? And in all three cases, will we release the beliefs that hold us back?

Research Professor Brené Brown studies courage, vulnerability, shame, and empathy. She wrote an extensive and informative piece of work called 'The Power of Vulnerability'.[13] We touched briefly on vulnerability earlier in this chapter, but it warrants a deeper look. Dr. Brown shares that vulnerability isn't a dark thing. It's powerful. She says it's the 'birthplace of innovation and change is essential to authenticity. Authenticity is the daily pattern of letting go of what we're supposed to be; it's setting boundaries'. Dr. Brown suggests buying a 'boundary ring' to be worn at all times. When someone requests something of you, she suggests spinning the ring three times before answering. Does

---

[13] Sounds True Publishing/soundstrue.com

this request appeal to me? If I say yes to this request, will I be doing it out of joy and interest or obligation? Saying no to a request that doesn't feel good to us can make us feel vulnerable to judgment about our decision. Who do you think you are? And that's an excellent question. Not in the sarcastic, shaming, judgmental sense. But in the discerning sense of 'Is this me?' Oftentimes, when we agree to do something out of obligation or fear of judgment—not willing to be vulnerable—we end up resenting both the person who made the request and the situation as well.

In her over twenty years of research, Dr. Brown found that most people believe they are not relevant enough. We live in a society that shouts, "BE MORE! DO MORE!" We wonder if our contributions to society are meaningful enough. We think that if we do monumental, public things we will be enough. And we look to others and outside circumstances to tell us how to achieve this greatness. But, as Dr. Brown points out, if 'how to' (be more, do more, contribute more, do monumental, public things) worked, we wouldn't be an obese, addicted nation. We get addicted to pleasures to compensate for the lack of true meaning and fulfillment that comes from being simply, uniquely, and authentically ourselves. We simply must allow ourselves our boundaries. We must look to our feelings to determine if a suggested or current plan of action is in line with our true desires and preferences – our grain in our own wood. One man who was electrocuted, died, and was revived said that before his near-death experience he never felt that his chosen line of work and what he did with his life was good enough. After coming back from the Other Side, he said he realized his purpose is not in what he does but who he is as a person. In his book 'After the Ecstasy, the

Laundry', Jack Kornfield says we must become independent of praise and blame. If we don't, we're like puppets. And what could be more inauthentic than a puppet? Do and be what you choose for the joy and satisfaction that it brings to you. Release yourself from the judgment of self and others. Being willing to be vulnerable opens us up to one of the greatest gifts we have – our intuition. Intuition has been referred to as our 'cosmic marching orders'.[14] If we listen to it, it will give us the direction for our personal path and purpose. If you find yourself constantly polling others for their opinions on what you should do, or acting before being inspired to act, according to Brené Brown and others, you are ignoring your own inner guidance. Being true to your own personal preferences and desires is as relevant as it gets. In this journey we call life, we need what the French call bon courage: good courage.

The emptiness, longing, and unfulfilled feelings we have don't come from something we don't have. They come from a self we've lost touch with, shares David Robert Ord in his book 'Your Forgotten Self'. I couldn't agree more. And I would add, they come from the self we didn't even know we were.

Taking the steps to figure out what thrills and fulfills you and then having the courage to act on it, again, is not selfish. I am reminded of a story of a father who was very busy trying to get some work done. His young son kept interrupting him, wanting his father to play with him. To buy some time, the father took a map of the world and tore it into many little pieces. He gave it to his son to put back together, knowing it

---

[14] "Book of Light" by Alexandra Solnado.

would take him a while. Before he knew it, the son had the map back in one piece. Astonished, his father asked him how he could have done that so fast. The son answered, "It was easy. On the other side of the map was a picture of a person. I put the person back together and the world was back together." Responsibility is responding to what makes your heart sing. When you do that, you are responding to who you are. And if we each can do that, the world will be the better for it. We're all unique. No one got everything. But we all got something. That's why we need each other.

"Why would you let the wonderful fact of your own existence go by?"[15]

Become Yourself

- Do the next joyful thing.
  - You know what you want by what you don't want
  - What's the essence behind the form?
  - Does it raise your vibrations?

- Become aware of and rewrite limiting beliefs.
  - If it bugs you, it's about you.
  - Blame is insane.
  - Notice what you notice.
  - Who built your box and why are you still in it?
  - Whispers become shouts.
  - Patterns point to their purpose.
  - If you want to know what you believe, look at what you have in your life. Your life always reflects your beliefs.

---

[15] "Atlas Shrugged" by Ayn Rand.

- Follow the grain in your own wood.
  - Does it raise your vibrations?
  - Define or be defined.

Chapter 5
Abracadabra

Ask and it will be given to you, seek and you will find,
knock and the door will be opened unto you.
– Jesus, from the Sermon on the Mount

IN THIS CHAPTER, we'll be delving into our desires and how and why they do or do not show up in our lives. The things we prefer in life are, again, the white squares of the crossword puzzle. They are the things we get to choose and fill in. To use the fan analogy, if the ribs of the fan are our AAA energy, our natural gifts, talents, and bents, the fabric of the fan is what we get to choose to express those unique and authentic energies.

The phrase 'abracadabra' is either of Hebrew or Aramaic origin. In Aramaic, it is 'avra kadavra', and its meaning is 'it will be created with my words'. It is believed that Jesus spoke Aramaic, and in Aramaic, the above quote from the Sermon on the Mount rounds out to 'ask without hidden motive and be surrounded by your answer, be enveloped by what you desire that your gladness be full'. [16] We are given the responsibility of asking for our desires. Once we ask, we are 'surrounded by our answers and enveloped by our desires'. For what purpose? "That our gladness be full." There's that happiness thing again.

Growing up in the Christian religion, I had heard, "Ask and you shall receive" many times. But I wasn't thinking about that one night, shortly after marrying Bruce. We were lying in bed, and I was strongly pondering the question, *How can I be parental without coming across as judgmental? How can I parent my kids without making them feel judged by me in the process?* I was really, really grappling with this because I sincerely wanted to be a good mom. I so desired an answer to this question that I woke Bruce up and asked him, "How can I be parental without being judgmental?" He answered, "Tammy, I don't know. I just need to sleep." Ugh. But it was true. He did need to sleep. I went to sleep that night with the question still burning in my heart. The following morning, I was driving and decided to turn on the radio, which I rarely did. Immediately, the voice on the radio said, "This morning we have a panel of twelve experts here to talk about the difference between being parental and judgmental." It felt so mystical and out of this world…abracadabra. I had asked and I had received. Unfortunately, at this time it seemed too surreal and scared me so much that I hastily turned the radio off and didn't even listen to the broadcast! Today, I can't believe I did that.

---

[16] "Spontaneous Evolution" by Bruce H. Lipton, PhD, and Steve Bhaerman.

As I said earlier, after marrying Bruce and having everything in life I ever wanted yet still feeling a void, I began earnestly searching for the meaning of life. I was questioning the religion of my upbringing and looking for answers to why we're here on Earth to begin with and what this thing called life was all about. Again, I was strongly asking for direction and guidance regarding these soul-wrenching questions. One day, while gearing up to play pick-up soccer, a fellow player approached me. I was surprised, to say the least, because this person was a veteran, talented player, and I was a nobody wannabe – new to the game and not in her circle. But here she was, kneeling in front of me. She told me that she had just read a book called Conversations with God and had a lot of questions about it. She thought I would be able to offer some insight and asked if I would meet her for lunch to discuss the book. I agreed, we met, and for once in my life, I listened more than I talked. I didn't offer the fundamental views of God that I had learned. Instead, I asked to borrow the book so I could read it and get back to her. She agreed, and that book by Neale Donald Walsch changed my spiritual paradigm one hundred and eighty degrees. It started me on my new journey of self and spiritual exploration. This woman, Michele, is now a dear friend of mine. She was led to reach out to me, someone she barely knew, and she listened to her intuition. By doing so, she brought an answer to my asking. Michele is also the friend who helped me design and decorate my bookstore, eleven years after introducing me to the book that changed my life. How fitting.

After reading Walsch, when I was in the middle of my eleven years on the couch, I read that human DNA is actually twelve-stranded, not two-stranded. This book was saying that what scientists were calling junk DNA was really ten more strands of DNA that were dormant. I was pondering this one day while riding my bike. I resonated with the idea but wasn't sure about it. I love DNA, and part of me wishes I had become a DNA researcher. As I was riding, I asked for a sign. If twelve-stranded DNA was something I should embrace, I needed a sign. I stopped at a red light and looked over at the car in the intersection to my right. The car had a license plate that read TAMMY12. Again? I could not believe it! This happened about thirteen years ago, and after a while, I started to question if I really saw that license plate. Was my mind playing tricks on me? Then, just last year, I shared this story with a friend. The next day, I was driving to my gym, and a car several cars ahead of me made a right turn. As it did, I noticed the license plate: TAMMY12.

These experiences truly seemed magical to me at the time. Abracadabra. I was creating as I asked. But how was this happening? I am a Scorpio, and true to the energy of this astrological sign, I want and need to know why and how things happen. I seek to get to the core of everything. For me, this means starting at the beginning. The basics.

The most fundamental place to start was with the fact that I am a human being living on Earth. With that comes certain givens.

Given #1: Variety

Everything and its opposite exist here on Earth. There are countless varieties of people, plants, animals, minerals, experiences, and emotions, just to name a few. There is much to explore here on Earth. The nature of our Universe is polarity. Everything is polarity.[17]

Given #2: Free Will

We all experience different levels of physical freedom, yet we all have the freedom to think our own thoughts, feel our own feelings, and know what would make us happy and fulfilled. In addition, having free will gives us the responsibility of asking for those desires. We are not robots, programmed and powerless to external control. Certainly, we can be controlled and dominated by other humans, and we often are. But free will means we have the freedom to want what we want. As Viktor Frankl points out in 'Man's Search for Meaning', "Forces beyond your control can take away everything you possess except your freedom to choose how you will feel."

Given #3: Choice

Variety plus free will leads to choices. We have the power to prefer. And the brains to make it happen. Humans share 99.4% of our DNA with chimpanzees. That 0.06% gives us the most evolved part of our brain – a large frontal cortex.[18] Having a large frontal cortex affords us intellect. The word 'intellect' comes from the root words 'intel' and 'legere'. Legere means 'to choose', and intel means 'between'.

---

[17] "What Tom Sawyer Learned from Dying" by Sidney Farr and Thomas Charles Sawyer.

[18] "Everything You Need to Know to Feel Go(o)d" by Dr. Candace Pert.

Humans have the ability to choose among all the variety that exists here on Earth.

Given #4: Emotions

Whatever we choose, "The endpoint of any experience is an emotion," says Dennis Prager in Happiness is a Serious Problem. Without emotions, we wouldn't care about choice. We choose based on what we believe will make us feel good or feel better. The lower one-third of our frontal cortex is called the orbitofrontal cortex, and it has to do with emotion. It comes into play when we are sizing up the reward/punishment, pleasure/pain aspects of a choice. People whose orbitofrontal cortex has been damaged cannot make decisions or choose. They can list pros and cons, but without emotions, they see little reason to choose at all.[19]

Perhaps you've never thought about the givens of being human. Maybe they even seem mundane and unimportant. I mean, they pretty much happen automatically. We're all humans here on Earth, experiencing variety, using our free will and emotions to choose what we desire. So why are many of us unfulfilled, unhappy, and feeling like life is a drain? The answer lies in Given #5.

Given #5: The vibrational basis of life

I can remember as a teenager my dad saying things to me like, "You think that table is solid, but it's really a bunch of vibrating particles with lots of space in between them." Or something like that. After all, I was a(n uninterested) teenager.

---

[19] "The Happiness Hypothesis" by Jonathan Haidt.

While science confirms that the basis of life is vibrational, I feel the need to go into depth about this particular 'Given' as it may not be as known or accepted as Givens #1–4.

In their book 'CosMos', philosopher of science Ervin Laszlo and PhD cosmologist Jude Currivan state, "Of the many competing theories that seek to describe the fundamentals of the physical universe, all describe its manifest nature in terms of vibrational excitations, which are essentially waveforms and these waveforms are electromagnetic." They are saying that what we see, what manifests, is first a vibration.

Inventor and engineer, Nikola Tesla, said that if you want to find the secrets of the Universe, think in terms of energy, frequency, and vibration.[20]

Dr. Hans Jenny, a medical doctor and researcher, studied the structure and dynamics of waves and vibrations extensively in the early to mid-twentieth century. He is known as the 'father of cymatics'. It is said of his work, "This book [Cymatics] and Hans Jenny's works are the documentation of the highest caliber of one of the most fundamental phenomena of matter – vibration." Dr. Jenny demonstrated the primacy of vibration. He found that the most basic, elemental, and foundational aspect of everything that exists is that everything vibrates. Leading researcher of, among other things, ancient knowledge, Freddy Silva says of Dr. Jenny, "Through Hans Jenny's ground-breaking work in cymatics, we have confirmation of the links between vibration, creation and the natural order of life."[21] Nothing happens on Earth without the

---

[20] "You Are a Badass" by Jen Sincero.

[21] "Secrets in the Fields" by Freddy Silva.

vibration that creates it. There is nothing more real than the vibrational basis of life…Given #5.

This theory is everywhere:

- In her book 'The Consciousness of the Atom', Tibetan teacher Alice A. Bailey defines evolution as the 'unfolding of a continuously increasing power to respond to vibrations'.
- Einstein: "All things are energy vibrating."
- There is an archaic Japanese word 'shindo'. It means 'vibrations and the way of the gods'.

You may be thinking, *Okay…so, everything vibrates. Why does that matter in a book about becoming empowered?*

Well, if everything vibrates that means you vibrate.

Scientists in the field of bioenergetics have shown that the frequency, or vibration, emitted from us is more unique than our fingerprints. Valerie Hunt, scientist and professor emeritus of physiological science at UCLA, spent twenty-five years using high-frequency instruments to measure the vibrations of humans. In her book, *'Infinite Mind'*, she states, "At the cutting edge of biological science is the understanding of vibrations" and that "thoughts are structured vibrations."

Stay with me…

The Princeton Engineering Anomalies Research (PEAR) lab did a study on dogs and their owners. Cameras were placed in the homes of the dog owners. It was observed that the dogs in the study all had a my-owner-is-coming-home routine they performed when they anticipated the return of their owner. The dogs did this religiously. What the researchers were interested in was not the coming home routine per se, but would the dogs perform the routine prior to the owners coming home at random times during the day instead of the expected time? They found that the dogs did indeed go through their routines before the owners' arrival, no matter what time the owners came home. Researcher Rupert Sheldrake studied this phenomenon extensively. Here are some stories from his book Dogs Who Know When Their Owners Are Coming Home:

I could always tell when my husband was on his way home because his dog would tell me! His business is approximately a ten-minute drive from home, and about fifteen minutes before he would arrive our Husky, Zero, would start to get agitated and excited. He'd follow me around and run back and forth to the front door waiting and looking...and waiting. Tony would come home at different times each day depending on his schedule, but it seems that Zero sensed when Tony was closing up and heading home.

This one from a soldier who was given sick leave but had not told his parents he was coming home:

When I arrived home Sandy, our Irish Terrier, was by the door and I was told that he had not moved from the door for two days, except to be fed and exercised. This was about the time I had been told I was getting sick leave. His behavior had naturally caused concern for my parents. When I unexpectedly arrived home, my mom said, "He knew you were coming. That explains it." This waiting at the door happened throughout my two and a half years of service in the army. Sandy would move to the door about forty-eight hours before I came home. My parents knew I was coming because Sandy knew.

Thoughts are vibrations that can be received. We think 60,000 to 70,000 thoughts per day. What we're thinking greatly matters, and we'll see why as we continue in this chapter.

Japanese researcher Dr. Masaru Emoto studied water crystals as receivers of thought vibrations. In his book, 'The Hidden Messages in Water', he shows pictures of water crystals from bottles of water that different thoughts and emotions had been directed onto. The emotion and thoughts of love directed onto a bottle of water produced crystals that looked like beautiful snowflakes. The emotion and thoughts of hate produced chaotic and dark unformed particles. One day, Dr. Emoto decided to perform a bold experiment. During a live lecture he was giving in Tokyo, he had a lab assistant stay in the lab, which was also in Tokyo. On his desk in his lab was a test tube filled with Tokyo city tap water. Through a live video feed, Dr. Emoto showed his lecture audience the lab assistant taking a specialized picture of the tap water. This photograph was then shown to the lecture participants. It was dark, chaotic, and unformed. Dr. Emoto had previously arranged for a group of three hundred people in Israel to join hands while circling a body of water, during this lecture time. They were led by a monk and instructed, at the right time, to hold a picture of the test tube of water that was back on the desk in Tokyo in their minds. They were to think and feel these three things about the water: Water, we love you. Water, we thank you. Water, we respect you. This having been completed, the lab assistant again photographed a sample of the Tokyo tap water. The photo was immediately shown to the people in the live lecture via the video feed. It was a beautiful crystal shaped like a snowflake. All things can receive and respond to the vibrations of thoughts and feelings, and when you consider that humans are seventy-five percent water, you have to wonder what the thoughts and feelings we have about ourselves are doing to us.

In his book, 'Breaking the Habit of Being Yourself', cellular biologist Glen Rein tells of a study he performed on the effects of thoughts and feelings on matter. He gave three groups of ten people a test tube of DNA. To the first ten, he gave the instructions to hold the test tube and create the feelings of love and appreciation for the DNA. For the second group, he asked them to do the same as the first group but to add the intentions/thoughts that the DNA would unwind and wind itself more. The third group was asked to hold the test tube of DNA and with their intentions/ thoughts ask it to unwind and wind itself more only. No emotion or feelings of love and appreciation were focused on the DNA by the third group. The results were that group two's DNA wound and unwound 25% more than the other two groups. Thoughts and intentions combined with feelings and emotions were more influential.

As stated above, all things can receive and respond to the vibrations of thoughts and feelings. On my couch reading 'Conversations with God', I could feel myself softening in a big way. As I said, the book was changing my spiritual paradigm completely. I could feel my whole energy shifting to a more compassionate and non-judgmental way of being. While reading, I noticed my daughter, who was sitting nearby but with her back to me, kept looking over her shoulder at me.

Suddenly, she burst into tears. She confessed to me that at a recent sleepover she and her friends had ordered a pizza to be delivered to an unexpecting neighbor. She hadn't told me about it because she was afraid she would get punished. Yes, I was relieved it wasn't something more dire. But the thing that hit me was that I believe my daughter could feel my vibrations changing while I read. She could feel that I was more open, less rigid, and it would be safe to share her story with me. She had picked up on the vibrations of my thoughts and feelings.

We vibrate. Everything vibrates.

Vibrations are transmitted and received.

Clincher: Vibrations attract their likeness.

The unique frequency or vibration being emitted by each of us is attracting experiences and circumstances that match that vibration.

In 1972, Dr. Candace Pert, whom I introduced earlier in the book, found the opiate receptor on our cells. This was a big deal in the 1970s. Scientists had been searching for the opiate receptor on our cells for nearly a hundred years. In her book 'Molecules of Emotion', Dr. Pert talks about preparing to search for the receptor by reading the one and only book on the subject, so little had been discovered. Even that book could only talk about the concept of an opiate receptor because, while there was evidence of said receptor, no proof had ever been found. The evidence that a receptor, kind of like a keyhole to a key, was a real thing was that when someone ingested opiates, a change occurred in the person. They had a change in their mood, psyche, and feelings. The opiates had to be getting into our cells or no change would have been affected. What Dr. Pert figured out (and I'm doing my best to relay the science here) was that the receptor wasn't always on the cell membrane. It only appeared when an opiate was in the vicinity. When this was the case, a part of the cell membrane would wiggle and change until it matched the vibration of the opiate, resonating with its vibration, and they were brought together through attraction. Dr. Pert referred to this as the opiate and the cell membrane having the same voice. Once this happened, the opiate could enter the cell through the now present receptor.

This is the same thing that happens when I play my piano in a room with two guitars. When I hit a certain note on the piano, both guitars begin playing the same note.

Vibrations attract their likeness.

- Sitting in a McDonald's drive-thru one day, the song 'Dream Weaver' came on the radio. I started singing and chair-dancing to it. My vibrations were all about the good feelings I was getting from that song. I looked up to see the car in front of me had the license plate DRMWVR.
- In my car driving one day, I had the strong urge to call my son and tell him that I loved him. I called and said, "Really I just called to say I love you." We chatted for a few minutes and at the end of the

conversation, Nic said, "Love you, too, Mom," just as I looked over at the car to my right and saw the license plate LVU2MOM.

We know vibrations attract their likeness, but how are our vibrations formed? Our thoughts cause us to feel an emotion. That emotion becomes our vibration. Dr. Valerie Hunt suggests that human emotions are the organizers of our energy fields. Change your emotion and change your vibration. Addiction expert Gabor Mate tells us in When the Body Says No, that psychoneuroimmunology is the science of the indissoluble unity of emotions and physiology; Dr. Pert was a psychoneuroimmunologist. What we feel, we vibrate – and that vibration is reflected in our experiences and our bodies.

The role our vibrations play in attracting what we experience in our lives is everything. Nothing happens without the vibration that precedes it. We accept gravity without question. We can't, and wouldn't want to, escape the effects of gravity. It is imperative that we accept the presence and properties of vibrations, too. You reap what you sow, vibrationally. The discoveries that show how everything vibrates and that those vibrations attract their likeness have actually redefined responsibility. We are each responsible for what shows up in our lives and bodies because we are each responsible for our emotions and, therefore, our vibrations.

A woman walked into my bookstore. She was perusing the books, clearly looking for something in particular.

Not finding it, she asked me, "Have you heard of Abraham?"

She was asking in kind of a mysterious way, almost whispering it. At first, I thought she was referring to Abraham the father of three religions. When she clarified that she was not looking for the biblical figure, I looked into it and found that a book called The Law of Attraction: The Basics of the Teachings of Abraham had been written and recently published by Esther and Jerry Hicks. They had also written Ask and It is Given. Intrigued, I ordered both books and read them. They say that everything is vibration and vibrations attract their likeness; you get what you think about; your thoughts and feelings create your experiences. This was the first time I was reading about creating your life experiences with your thoughts and emotions on purpose. It was what I had been doing, unknowingly, with my experiences with the radio and license plates, and with my friend Michele. My strong desires, my strong feelings were attracting their likeness. Everything the Abraham-Hicks © [22] books were saying made sense to me, but I knew I had to try it out 'on purpose' and test their 'Law of Attraction' before I could fully believe in it.

So it was that on a Monday morning, I chose a situation to focus on that I wanted to be different. It was near and dear to my heart because it was breaking my son's heart. Therefore, there was a lot of emotion involved in my desire to create a new situation using my thoughts, feelings, and emotions – my vibrations. The situation at hand was this: My son, Nic, was in his senior year of high school. He was slated to be a starter on the varsity basketball team. Nic loved basketball. He had injured his ankle before the start of the season, and he had to heal before he could play. Once his ankle had healed, however, the coaches were not playing him.

---

[22] Abraham-Hicks.com. support@abraham-hicks.com

He didn't understand why. He asked the coaches but did not get an answer that satisfied him. It really was tough on him, and therefore, on me. This is what I did: I quieted my mind and got into a meditative state. I can honestly say I've never been quite as 'dreamy' before or since that morning. I visualized and felt the wonderful feeling of the head basketball coach coming to Nic and saying, "Nic, I'm sorry we haven't been playing you. I talked with the assistant coach. We really value your three-point shot, and we're going to start playing you."

I have to emphasize how I was 'all in' during this visualization. Afterward, I told myself that if that scenario did not play out by the end of that day, I could not believe in the Law of Attraction I'd read about. If this conversation did not take place on that day between Nic and his coach, I couldn't believe that I could deliberately create a vibration with my thoughts, emotions, and intentions and have that same vibration come back to me. Looking back, I can't believe I was so bold as to expect results that day!

Nic came home for lunch on the same day I held my intentioned vibration meditation. Nothing. Nic came home after school and made his usual trek to his bedroom. My heart and hopes crashed. I was so very disappointed. I really wanted to believe that thoughts can turn into things. Suddenly, Nic stopped in his tracks and said, "Mom! I almost forgot to tell you. Coach sought me out right before school ended today. I was in the bathroom, and he actually came looking for me. He said, 'Nic, I'm sorry we haven't been playing you. I talked with the assistant coach. We really value your three-point shot, and we're going to start playing you'."

My eyes filled with tears. I was so happy for my son. But more than that I was blown away by what he had just said to me and what those words meant. Let me clarify that I don't believe one can create so directly another person's reality, nor should they. I'm not really sure how it was able to happen in this experience except to say that, perhaps, it was my reality, too. I had tapped into my vibrations more in that moment than I ever had, and it felt like magic. Abracadabra!

Today I firmly believe that thoughts turn into things. The frequency or vibration coming from us, being broadcast from us, attracts its likeness. We can call it, as Abraham-Hicks © do, 'the Law of Attraction'. It has also been called the Law of Vibration. The ancients called it the Law of Power. Whatever you call it, I believe it was set into motion by the All That Is. It truly is our power…asking and receiving.

Okay, you say. I vibrate with getting a new car. I vibrate with being rich. I vibrate with being in a wonderful relationship. I have been living the variety that Earth offers. I have decided on what I prefer. Why are these things not happening?

Because the biggest contributor to our overall vibration is our beliefs. When we were young and forming those beliefs, they got downloaded into our subconscious minds. That's where they live. Beliefs like money doesn't grow on trees, I'm not worthy to be adored, money is the root of all evil, it's not okay to be selfish, and it takes hard work and sacrifice to get nice things override the conscious thoughts of wanting a new car, being rich, and wanting a great relationship. If there's something in life that you desire but aren't getting, look for a limiting belief that is adding more to your vibration than your conscious desire is. When the book 'The Secret' came out, its message was love yourself, think positive thoughts, and those positive things will manifest in your life. I think the book fell short, though, by not speaking to the influence our beliefs have on our vibration much more so than positive affirmations or words. I wonder if that is what 'ask without hidden motive'[23] is referring to – those limiting beliefs?

In her book 'Bringers of the Dawn', Barbara Marciniak makes the statement that the 'first and final tenet is that thought creates'. As already mentioned, we think 60,000–70,000 thoughts per day. Ninety percent of them are the same ones we thought yesterday. Again, that is because of our beliefs; these are so ingrained in our subconscious that we can't easily shirk or ignore them. As Abraham-Hicks © say, a belief is just a thought you keep thinking. Our beliefs lead to our thoughts, which cause our emotions, which form our vibrations, which create what shows up in our lives. The book CosMos informs us that the science of physics, which seeks to understand the fundamental nature of the physical universe, is in turmoil but the scientists of physics are clear on one thing: we can no longer separate mind from matter. We are being asked to recognize that we are energetic beings whose thoughts, feelings, and emotions create the world we meet. When we can consciously choose our thoughts and emotions, we are in our power. The past is gone, and the future will be created from how you feel right now.

You get what you think about.

---

[23] Jesus's 'Sermon on the Mount'.

Become Yourself

- Do the next joyful thing.
  - You know what you want by what you don't want.
  - What's the essence behind the form?
  - Does it raise your vibrations?

- Become aware of and rewrite limiting beliefs.
  - If it bugs you, it's about you.
  - Blame is insane.
  - Notice what you notice.
  - Who built your box, and why are you still in it?
  - Whispers become shouts.
  - Patterns point to their purpose.
  - If you want to know what you believe, look at what you have in your life. Your life always reflects your beliefs.

- Follow the grain in your own wood.
  - Does it raise your vibrations?
  - Define or be defined.

- Abracadabra!
  - Ask and you shall receive.
  - I create with my vibration.

Chapter 6
Drop the Oars

A 113-year-old Floridian was asked the secret to his
longevity. His answer:
When it rains, I let it.

RESISTANCE. IT'S what prevents us from receiving what we
desire. If what you want and are asking for is not showing up
in your life, you have some form of resistance to it
manifesting. Most likely, it is a limiting belief. This is why it
is imperative that we do the work of chapter Three. We need
to see the patterns in our lives, figure out what beliefs are
behind them, and rewrite those self-limiting beliefs into self-
affirming beliefs. When something we desire, including the
wishes for peace, happiness, purpose, ease—not just physical
things—isn't showing up in our experience, we know the
vibration coming from us isn't matching those desires. Our
beliefs, thoughts, and/or feelings are causing resistance in our
vibration. I used to use this analogy with my clients: You are
the quarterback of a football team. Your goal is to score a
touchdown. Eleven people are trying to stop you, resisting
your efforts. If those eleven people removed their helmets,

you would see that they are all you. You and your vibration are the only things stopping you from reaching your goal.

Not getting what you desire is one way of knowing that your vibration is not a match to what you desire. Another way to know you are resisting is by having negative emotions. Feeling negative emotions such as depression, victimization, frustration, boredom—any form of disempowerment—is a way of knowing you are in resistance to your desires.

'Does it raise my vibrations?' is a very good question to ask ourselves. We are here on Earth in our human bodies, living among all the variety and choosing our preferences. It is impossible to not do this. As we go about our days, we observe all that is going on and we instantly (consciously or unconsciously) know what we want by what we don't want. Now the question becomes, are we going to allow or resist those preferences and desires? If our fans are wide open—we're feeling good, inspired, joyful, which means our vibrations are high—we are allowing and welcoming the fulfillment of what we want. Feeling good is the key to creating the life we want. It's not the other way around. Having the life we want in order to feel good is backward. The happiness and good feelings are what allow our desires to flow.

In this chapter, we'll be discussing how we can lower our resistance and enhance our allowing. This is how we can be a vibrational match to what we want in our lives. I give the Abraham-Hicks © materials credit for most of the analogies and sayings I will be using. They said it well and, well, they said it.

LOWERING RESISTANCE

Opening up our vibrations and having little resistance can bring solutions.

Dr. Candace Pert tells of being a presenter at a conference on AIDS; her lab, at the time, was working on a cure for AIDS, and she was there to share their progress. Despite their significant progress, there was one thing that was eluding them. Sitting in the audience, waiting for her turn to speak, Dr. Pert was moved to tears by a presentation of the devastation that AIDS was causing in New York City, San Francisco, and Provincetown, Massachusetts. Her heart was blown wide open. Her vibration was pure. She was up next to present her data. In the middle of her talk, out of her mouth came the elusive thing that would help complete their cure! Dr. Pert says of this experience, "But I did allow myself to be moved by compassion for people suffering from AIDS and that was the key to me hearing my own inner voice."

Compassion is a very effective vibration cleanser, helping to rid our vibrations of the resistance to what we seek. Here is another story that speaks to compassion lowering resistance. My son, Nic, was desiring a raise in his job. Nic felt that his contributions were worth more than he was being compensated for monetarily. At the same time, he and his boss were at odds over how to run the business, and Nic found himself being (privately) critical of his boss's decisions. No raise was coming. He would discuss his frustrations with his sister, Rachael, and me. We both advised him to change his attitude/vibrations and things would change. He understood this intellectually—if it bugs you, it's about you—but he was unable to shake the feeling that he was being devalued. These negative, victim feelings were adding resistance to his vibration. Then one night, as Nic says 'out of the blue', he became overwhelmed with compassion for his boss. He got how it must feel difficult and scary to have all the risk of owning a business and supporting a family. He was also, like Dr. Pert, moved to tears. This was on a Wednesday night. That very Friday, Nic's boss looked at him and 'out of the blue' said, "Your raise starts next week." Nic experienced how changing your vibration, lowering your resistance, can change a situation. He shared this story with me, saying that he now knew what Rachael and I had been saying. This is a great example of how words don't teach. Nic had to experience it for himself.

Quieting your mind is also a good way to lower resistance and allow solutions. Meditation and sleep are two ways to do this.

Elias Howe, the inventor of the lockstitch sewing machine, was frustrated because in his prototype the thread kept bunching up and getting jammed. He could not figure out why. Then one night, he had a dream in which he was suddenly surrounded by tribal people with big sticks in their hands. They were trying to kill him. They had spears with a hole in the end and they moved them up and down. They did this over and over. He immediately knew, upon waking, that this was the answer to his thread problem. In his prototype, he had put the hole for the thread in the middle of the needle. He now knew the hole needed to be at one end. He made that change, and the sewing machine worked beautifully.[24]

Professional golfer Jack Nicklaus was going through a rough spot with his golf game. He was consistently shooting

---

[24] Newenglandhistoricalsociety.com.

scores in the high seventies. In 1964, he told a San Francisco Chronicle reporter, "I had a dream and it was about my golf swing. I was hitting them pretty well in the dream, and all at once, I realized I wasn't holding the club the way I've actually been holding it lately. I've been having trouble collapsing my right arm, taking the club-head away from the ball, but I was doing it perfectly in my sleep. So when I came to the course yesterday morning, I tried it the way I did in my dream and it worked. I shot a 68 yesterday and a 65 today."[25]

After struggling to come up with a plot for a while, novelist Robert Louis Stevenson was given the inspiration for one of modern literature's most famous works, 'The Strange Case of Dr. Jekyll and Mr. Hyde', in a dream.[26]

Inventors like Thomas Edison and Benjamin Franklin would get stumped while working on various inventions. They had a way to quiet their minds, stop trying so hard, and receive their solutions. It wasn't anything complicated or unique to their skill sets. They would simply sit in a chair to relax, holding a hairbrush or other object in one hand. As they relaxed enough to almost fall asleep, the hairbrush/object would fall out of their hands onto the floor, bringing them back to full consciousness. This 'reset' of sorts would allow them access to previously blocked insights and to redirect the flow of their thoughts as to how to move on and bring the inventions to fruition.

What you resist persists

---

[25] "On Par: The New York Times" golf blog.
[26] Study.com.

Mystic Almine shares in her book Life of Miracles, "It is a Universal Law that you strengthen what you oppose." This works for building muscles, where you want resistance to make something bigger. In trying to create the life experiences and situations you desire, resistance only serves to grow those undesired things in your life. If you find you're getting the same old, same old, despite wanting something different, know that you have resistance in your vibration. The good news is that everything you want is of a high vibration. Great relationships, abundance, ease, fulfilling careers, healthy and fit bodies – these all feel good and, therefore, are of a high vibration. There is not one specific high vibration for a great relationship, one for abundance, or one for health and fitness. All things wanted are allowed to flow into our lives as long as we have a good, high vibration without resistance.

What follows are strategies for lowering resistance and maintaining good vibrations. We simply must find a way to feel good—be a wide-open fan—even when, or especially when shit hits that fan. As Florence Scovel Shinn says in The Game of Life, "One's ship comes in over calm seas."

- Drop the Oars

Abraham-Hicks © gives the analogy of our desires being a fast-moving stream. All we need to do is get into the boat and go with the flow. If we pick up the oars, turn the boat upstream, and feverishly fight the current, we're resisting our desires. I labeled one oar 'how' and the other 'judgment'. Ask and you shall receive does not tell us that we get what we want by fighting for it, sweating over it, or wearing ourselves out trying to figure out how to get it. It's just ask and receive.

113

"How" we receive is not up to us. Let the Universe and the All That Is surprise and delight you. Abraham-Hicks © tells the story of a woman who desperately wanted to attend one of their conferences, but she could not afford it. She didn't fret or ask others for money. She simply stayed open and non-resistant, pure within her desire to go to a conference. One day, she and a friend were out for a walk and this woman noticed something shiny in the grass. Picking it up, she saw it was a large earring. Although it looked like a diamond earring, it was big, and she and her friend felt it was most likely cubic zirconium. She took it to a jeweler who confirmed it was, indeed, a diamond – valued at $9,000!

My stepdaughter, Amy, mentioned to us about a year ago that she wanted an electric bike, an e-bike. It wasn't in her budget, and she wasn't obsessing over getting it. She simply wanted one. Recently, a friend of Amy's had her garage broken into, and this friend's e-bike was stolen. Insurance paid for a new one. Amy's friend was out riding her new e-bike when a man rode up next to her on her stolen e-bike! She said, "Hey! That's my bike!" The man admitted he had stolen it and agreed to go with her to the police station. She got the stolen bike back, and since she didn't need two e-bikes, she gave the returned e-bike to Amy. Amy had to make a few repairs, but she got an electric bike with no effort on her part. Just the unresisted desire.

Trying to figure out 'how' our desires manifest in our lives lowers our vibration and keeps us a vibrational mismatch to the things we want. This is absolutely not to say that we don't take action toward a goal. Dropping the oars and lowering resistance allows inspiration to float into our consciousness. Inspired action is fun and effortless. Inspired action, while perhaps physically demanding, will never be energy draining. According to Abraham-Hicks ©, the number one flawed premise of humans is 'the more you do the more you're worth'. It's not about doing. It's about inspired doing. A few years ago, I wanted to lose twenty pounds. I got the inspired thought to look into how bodybuilders eat. I acted on that inspiration, followed their way of eating, and even got some friends to join me. We had a blast getting together and planning new meals to fit our regime. Twenty weeks later I was twenty pounds thinner. And it was fun and effortless.

Now on to the 'judgment' oar. Earth, as we've talked about, is full of variety. The Abraham-Hicks © material calls it contrast. Without contrast we couldn't know what we want. If everything was blue, we wouldn't even know blue. We need contrast in order to define our choices. The Abraham-Hicks © material also likens the contrast and variety to a well-stocked kitchen. Every ingredient you can imagine is in this kitchen. If you want to make an apple pie, you will go into the kitchen and choose apples, sugar, flour, etc. You don't judge the beef roast or red peppers for being there, as well. They simply aren't what you want. Judgment is a big contributor to resistance and lowered vibrations. I'm not saying to not be discerning. If something is not for you, simply say, "No thank you." If you're not a vibrational match to it, it can't manifest in your reality anyway. If you judge it, however, it means you're fighting against it, and what you resist persists. You get what you vibrate. If you're involved in the war on cancer, terrorism, poverty, or whatever, you're keeping the vibration of cancer, terrorism, and poverty alive. Of course, no one wants cancer, terrorism, or poverty, but fighting against them keeps them active. And remember you know what you want by what you don't want. Not wanting cancer, terrorism, and poverty means you want good health, peace, and abundance. Focusing on these will bring more of these.

Be happy in the gap. [27]We do reap what we vibrationally sow. Just like it takes time for a sown seed to turn into a flower

> Have a desire → gap of time until it manifests → stay happy in the gap → desire manifests → new desire → gap of time until it manifests → stay happy in the gap → desire manifests → new desire

or a stalk of corn, it takes time for the seeds of our desires to show up in our lives. The key is to be happy in that gap of time. If we worry or focus on it not having manifested yet, we are, again, a vibrational mismatch to what we desire. Abraham-Hicks © example of this is that you decide you're going to drive from Phoenix, Arizona, to San Diego, California. You don't get halfway there and turn back around and go back to Phoenix because you're not in San Diego yet. You know the journey takes time. You have a destination/desire, and you know you're on your way to it. There is just a gap of time between when we leave (have a desire) and when we get there (see the desire flow into our lives). And, the thing is, we spend ninety percent of our lives in that gap! One desire's fulfillment leads to a new desire. Over and over. That's how we expand and evolve. If we cease to have desires, we cease to exist.

---

[27] Abraham-Hicks ©podcast

- Don't look back – unless you want to go there. Your GPS in your car never asks you where you've been before it tells you how to get to where you want to go. It guides you from where you are right now. Regrets, guilt, and should-haves keep us in a low vibration. Our past can and does inform our present, but each new moment is a new opportunity to choose again.

- Focus is magnetic to form. You get what you focus on. Pay attention to what you're thinking about. Are you focused on your dreams or the lack of them? I had a playful client, and to bring this point home to him I gave him a nerf gun. I held up two targets. One target read, "Great, exciting, and lucrative career." The other target said, "Boring, mundane job I currently have." On which one did he want to shoot the bullseye? Of course, the great and exciting career target.

When focusing on something you want, it is a good idea to be as specific as you can believe. For instance, the above client could believe there was a great, exciting, and lucrative career out there for him. But if we filled in details such as 'It'll happen tomorrow', or 'I'll make a million dollars a year', or 'I'll have more free time than I actually work', and he had trouble believing those things, we would introduce resistance. Be as specific as you can with details if you don't feel any resistance while doing so. If you do feel resistance, or non-belief, as Abraham-Hicks © says, go more general.

Feeling the feeling of having your desires met is critical to focus. Feel the breeze blowing in your face while riding in that new convertible you want. Feel the love you have for the baby you desire. And, as Gandhi said, "Be the peace you want to see in the world." Be in the vibration of what you desire.

- Beat the drum of what you want. [28] This is similar to focus is magnetic to form. I used to give my clients an actual drum. I would ask them to beat the drum while thinking of things in their life that weren't working for them. They could barely bring themselves to touch the drum. When they did, it was always a slow, monotonous, uninspired beat. Then I asked them to beat the drum while thinking of unlimited abundance, amazing relationships, feeling fulfilled and passionate, of ease and flow. Immediately, their vibrations were raised and they smiled while beating out an upbeat rhythm. Some of them even danced along. Most of us, without realizing it, are beating the drum of what we have, not of what we want. Beating the drum of what you have just gets you more of the same. It doesn't take any more time or preparation to choose to focus on and feel the feeling of having what you want in your life than it does to focus on and feel the feeling of what you already have. It's a choice of where you put the 60,000–70,000 thoughts you have every day. Your thoughts create your feelings, and your feelings create your vibration, and your vibration attracts your

---

[28] Abraham-Hicks © podcast

118

experiences. Be aware of your mood and of how you feel. If you're uninspired and disempowered, you're beating the drum of 'what is'. Beat the drum of what you want and feel the feeling of it. You might even dance.

- Release the outcome. This is akin to dropping the oar of 'how'. When you plant a seed of corn, do you make it grow? Once planted, all you can do is nurture the seed. Your job is to care for it, love it, and relax. How can the All That Is surprise and delight us if we have to control the outcome of everything? Plant the seeds of your desires, be happy in the gap, and release the outcome.

- Choose thoughts and things that already feel good. ll: The only reason we want anything in life is because we think we will feel better in the having of it.:ll

If you're not a reader of music, you might not know what the ll: and the :ll at the beginning and end of the above saying are. They are repeat signs. If these symbols are written into a piece of music, the musician is meant to repeat the music that is between the two symbols. It bears repeating, over and over, that if the goal is feeling good, choosing thoughts and things that already feel good makes sense. I once asked my elderly, and somewhat demented, father-in-law what the secret to being happy was. He said, "Wake up and be happy!"

Many of us think, *If I only had _____, I would be happy.* Knowing now how vibrations work, we can see the flaw in that way of thinking. Happy begets happy. Vibrations attract their likeness. If you're not already happy, you can't attract happy things. Get happy first, and then those things you think you can't be happy without will flow into your life. Author Mike Dooley made popular the saying, "Thoughts become things." From his book *'Life on Earth'*: "Happiness isn't a crop you harvest when your dreams come true. It's the fertilizer that makes them come true faster."

If there's a situation in your life that you can't be happy while thinking about, don't think about it. Think about your dog, a good book, or a glass of wine. The other day, I asked my mom how she was feeling being in the midst of the Covid-19 pandemic. She answered that she was feeling good because she was choosing to feel good. We all have that choice.

- Tell it like it is if you like it like it is. Abracadabra. You create as you speak. If you're talking about something, it's active in your vibration. Whatever you talk about will increase in your life.

It's very unnerving for me to be a part of most conversations. People talk about things that aren't going their way. Most people are not talking about their dreams and passions, or what a wonderful life they have. It's almost like we think that would be bragging. I realize that we all go through things that we need to process, and talking to others can help us do that. But if typical conversations are a pattern of complaining, expressing worries or fears, gossiping, or just negative in general, they are inviting more of the same.

Whenever I have guests, I put out a bowl of mixed nuts. One day, my son noticed that most of the cashews, walnuts, pecans, and macadamia nuts were gone. What remained were peanuts. He said, "Mom, nobody likes peanuts." We must stop focusing on the peanuts in our lives. Unless, of course, we want more peanuts. What does a bowl full of peanuts cause you to desire? Focus on that.

I used the above sayings and tools with my clients to help them remember that lowering resistance was the way to allow feel-good things to manifest. Here are a few more tools for being a vibrational match to your desires:

- Appreciate the things in your life that are working. Appreciation is the closest vibration to the highest vibration that exists – total unconditional love. Actively appreciate. Look at the stars, your child, your mate, a tree…and say thank you and feel the love. Keep an appreciation journal. Sketch the things you appreciate. Anything you can do to focus on the things you appreciate will raise your vibration.
- Meditate – turn your mind off for fifteen minutes a day. Have no agenda. Turning your thoughts off will automatically raise your vibration. Turning your thoughts off allows for inspirational ideas to flow into your consciousness. While meditating, you may get the inspiration to clean out a closet. Doesn't sound too inspiring? While cleaning out the closet you find some important documents you need but had no idea where they could be found. The inspiration may seem mundane, but follow it. And be curious.
- Visualize. Imagination is a priceless tool for creating. I have heard that our imagination is actually the scissors cutting out our desired experiences.
- Be kind.
- Come from love.

- Find the positive aspects of any situation that is troubling you. (Example: The Covid-19 pandemic is troubling, to say the least. There are, however, some positive aspects to it. The air and waterways are getting cleaner. Businesses are being creative and innovative; developing processes that will be useful even after the pandemic is over. People are forced to do things in ways they never would have thought about that are even better than the old ways.) I have found this to be an extremely helpful tool for changing my negative, worrisome, and fearful thoughts. I label the top of a legal pad The Positive Aspects of (whatever situation I am struggling to come to peace with). Underneath this, I write 25 positive aspects of this situation. It takes thought, but it never fails to change my mood and vibration.

- Choose your feelings. I imagine that I have a barn full of horses. Each horse has a different name. Names like Peaceful, Curious, Anticipation, Easy Flowing, Surprise Me, Perfect Timing. I currently have about sixty imaginary horses. I choose which horse I want to ride in each segment of my day by how I want to feel and vibrate during that part of my day. If I am concerned about something that is going on that day, I might choose to ride Curious. Feeling curious is a much higher vibration than feeling concerned.

- Notice your emotional posture. Do you often find yourself in warrior mode? Fear? Ease? Compassion? Defensiveness? What is your default emotional posture?

Use any of the above tools and processes that resonate with you. Will they work 100% of the time? Maybe…Maybe not…Probably not…Again, life is difficult. Many, many factors and beliefs contribute to our overall vibration. But I 100% believe that no matter where you are in your life, these means are invaluable for your expansion.

I am reminded of a popular Native American story I'm sure many are familiar with. A grandfather tells his grandson that there are two wolves constantly fighting inside of him. One wolf is negative – he is anger, envy, sorrow, regret, greed, arrogance, self-pity, resentment, false pride, and ego. The other is positive – he is joy, love, hope, serenity, humility, kindness, empathy, generosity, truth, and compassion.

The boy asks his grandfather, "Which wolf wins?" "The one you feed," replies the grandfather.

Here's another story: A man dies and finds himself in front of St. Peter at the Pearly Gates to Heaven. St. Peter takes him by the hand and escorts him into Heaven. The man notices there are many, many rooms. Each room has a name over the doorway. Mary, Todd, Elizabeth, John, etc. In each room, there are boxes. Some rooms have a lot of boxes. Some rooms have a few boxes. Some rooms have no boxes. The man asks St. Peter, "What's with the boxes?"

St. Peter answers, "Oh, those are full of all the things the people on Earth are asking for but not letting in."

According to Abraham-Hicks ©, the true premise of life is, "The better you feel, the more you allow." Get happy. Feel good. Don't leave any boxes in Heaven.

Become Yourself

- Do the next joyful thing.
    - You know what you want by what you don't want.
    - What's the essence behind the form?
    - Does it raise your vibrations?

- Become aware of and rewrite limiting beliefs.
    - If it bugs you, it's about you.
    - Blame is insane.
    - Notice what you notice.
    - Who built your box and why are you still in it?
    - Whispers become shouts.
    - Patterns point to their purpose.
    - If you want to know what you believe, look at what you have in your life. Your life always reflects your beliefs.

- Follow the grain in your own wood.
    - Does it raise your vibrations?
    - Define or be defined.

- Abracadabra!
    - Ask and you shall receive.
    - I create as I speak.

- Drop the oars.
    - What you resist persists.
    - Be happy in the gap.
    - Don't look back. (Unless you want to go there.)

o   Focus is magnetic to form.
o   Beat the drum of what you want.
o   Release the outcome.
o   Choose your mood.
o   Tell it like it is if you like it like it is.

Chapter 7
Reflections

He thinks in secret and it comes to pass
Environment is his looking glass.
— James Allen from As a Man Thinketh

THROUGHOUT MY journey to become myself, I learned to look at things differently. The greater my awareness became, the more my way of seeing the world and life evolved. Awareness gave rise to perception. Broadening my perspective changed the way I see the meaning of life, why we're here, and what it's all about.

Consider this: We live in a three-dimensional world. One in which a ball looks to us like a ball. That same ball in a zero dimension would look like a dot on a page. In one dimension, it would appear as a straight line on a page. In two dimensions, a circle on a piece of paper. And, again, in three dimensions, it looks like a spherical ball. More expansive perspectives result in us seeing the exact same object in more fullness and depth. It's like the familiar story of blindfolded men who have never seen an elephant, each touching a different part of the elephant. The man touching the trunk describes an elephant as a muscular, tube-like animal. The man touching the ears says an elephant is a broad, floppy disk-like creature. It's only when they take off their blindfolds that they can see the whole elephant – the bigger picture.

At the beginning of my seeking, all I wanted to know was my purpose. I just 'knew' I had one, and if I could figure out what it was, I would be happy. Period. A zero-dimensional ball. I then was told that my purpose would be born out of my passions and what made me joyful. New viewpoint…Expanded awareness…I had always thought my purpose was something outside of me, not necessarily connected to what I was passionate about or what made me happy. Now I had something to work with, a path to follow. Another dimension! The dot had become a straight line.

Following what I was passionate about brought me to the discovery of limiting beliefs. More expansion…Increased consciousness, which is just another way of saying increased awareness. Prior to this knowledge, my limiting beliefs lived in my subconscious. I simply wasn't conscious, or aware, that I had them. My experience of wrestling with doing what made me fulfilled and able to thrive, combined with the books I came across that explained limiting beliefs to me, prompted me to figure out what mine were and choose differently. Now I was a person who knew my purpose was directly related to my joy and that I had beliefs that no longer served me. I was the same person, but with a wider viewpoint. A more evolved perspective. A circle.

Discovering and embracing my natural gifts and energies—my archetypes, astrology, and ancestry—helped me to see and become even more of myself. It empowered me to realize and own my uniqueness. It showed me why I was passionate, interested, and intrigued by certain experiences

127

and journeys, and not by others. Doing my next joyful thing, choosing the beliefs I wanted, and becoming more aware of my unique energies and talents took me to yet another dimension. One in which I could be fully me. I could be the ball.

Living in a three-dimensional world makes it easy for us to visualize a ball. After all, a ball is a three-dimensional object. We can see it, touch it, smell it, hear it bounce, and, if we choose, taste it. What's maybe not so easy to accept about our three-dimensional world is the subject of vibrations. Although everything in our world is a translation of a vibration—EKGs of the heart, EEGs of the brain, sound, feeling a vibe, thoughts—the conversation regarding vibrations is a fairly new one. Despite scientific evidence telling us so, it's still hard to wrap our heads around the fact that everything is energy vibrating and that those vibrations attract their likeness. Perhaps it's not so difficult to accept those facts on a purely scientific basis, but when applied to our lives – we vibrate and therefore attract to ourselves those people and situations that match our vibration – that acceptance may be questioned. Of course, this is nothing new. Humanity has been reluctant, to put it mildly, to embrace new scientific discoveries that go against traditional beliefs. When Carl Jung discovered synchronicity, he had to wait twenty years to make it public due to the consciousness of the time. Now it is common knowledge. Galileo was placed under house arrest and accused of heresy when he made public his telescopic observations that the Earth was not the center of the universe. The population at large would simply not accept that the Earth and other planets revolve around a stationary sun. But Galileo had a new way of seeing the same old thing. He had the telescope and that broadened his awareness of the universe. Up until 2,000 years ago, the world was believed to be flat. New technology brings new awareness. The key to all forms of transformation is increased awareness. Yet it's not easy to change a paradigm.

A four-dimensional spatial view of a ball is an interesting thing. As I understand it, a ball viewed in four dimensions would still look like a three-dimensional ball, but the added aspect would be that nothing would be hidden from view. One could see what's behind the ball without actually being behind the ball. To accomplish this in 3D, we would have to use a mirror.

We are operating under the Laws of Attraction and Reflection.[29] Reflections. To return to Colin Tipping's quote: "If you want to know what you believe/vibrate look at what you have in your life. Your life always reflects your beliefs/vibrations." In order to experience anything, you must be resonating at the same frequency. Our beliefs create our thoughts, and our thoughts create our emotions. All of these combine to make up our vibrational essence. That vibrational essence is being reflected back to us through our relationships, experiences, situations, emotions, and bodies. All of these are mirrors reflecting back to us what we are emitting vibrationally.

I shared earlier in the book how our bodies reflect our emotions through my story of the bookstore buddy with the kidney stone and my informal client who had spinal and foot issues. To learn more about how our bodies are mirrors

---

[29] "The Great Human Potential: Walking in One's Own Light" by Tom Kenyon and Wendy Kennedy.

showing us what we are vibrating, I recommend Candace Pert's audiobook Your Body is Your Subconscious Mind and Louise Hay's book You Can Heal Your Life.

Experiences like relationships, money, career, fun, adventure, and abundance, to name a few, all show us whether or not we are a vibrational match to our desires. If you have what you desire to experience in life, you know that your beliefs, thoughts, and emotions are aligned with your desires. A lack of anything you wish to have in your life gives you the awareness that you are resistant in some way and aren't allowing those wishes to manifest. Our experiences are mirrors, reflecting back to us what we are thinking and therefore feeling and therefore vibrating.

Our emotions are also mirrors. I saved emotions as mirrors for last because they are two-way mirrors. On one hand, they are indicators. They indicate alignment with your desires. When you're feeling empowered, joyful, at peace, at ease, interested, flowing, satisfied, and eager for more, you are in alignment with what you want in life. Feeling emotions such as disempowerment, depression, boredom, anger, or being stuck let you know you are misaligned with what you want. It's essential to follow the feelings you're experiencing to know if you're a vibrational match to your desires or not.

On the other hand, emotions can also create alignment or misalignment. Not getting what you want? Get happy. Stay satisfied and eager for more. Then watch as your happy, high vibration attracts feel-good things into your life. Stay focused on what's not happening in your life, or on what is happening that you don't want, and watch as more of those experiences become your reality. If feeling good is the goal, is it such a hardship to feel good no matter what? If the only reason we want anything is because we believe we will feel better in the having of it, feeling better and good regardless of what's happening makes all kinds of sense.

Awareness and self-empowerment are inseparable. Self-awareness leads to self-empowerment.

It is imperative that we see things for what they ask of us. Having feedback on what we're putting out vibrationally allows us to change our vibration if we want to attract something different in our lives. It puts us in charge of our life experiences. I believe this is reflected in, believe it or not, video games.

When video games first came out, I didn't understand the huge draw they had on our kids. They were obsessed. I found them to be frustrating. They came with no instructions. You learned through experience what was going to get you to the next level or get you killed. Now I see video games as a reflection of our growing awareness of how life works. Life is not a game of chance like Candyland, in which only the luck of the draw determines your fate. A game in which there is a winner and losers. Life is not just a game of skill like chess, in which the more skilled player wins and the other loses. Life is like a video game. You get no instructions. Interestingly, you do get a 'joy' stick – not a 'misery' stick. The game, like life, has levels, and the purpose of the game is to learn through experience how to advance to the highest level of the game. You become more aware. The only thing you are trying to beat is the game. The end goal is to have more control over the game than the game has over you. This is why I became a self-empowerment life coach. I wanted to guide others to have more control over their lives than their lives had over them.

If life is a game, the scoreboard is how you feel. This book is all about the evolution of feeling good from being conditionally accepted by others to feeling good through unconditionally embracing our unique and authentic selves. Like Dorothy in the Wizard of Oz, our journey to self-worth requires a Scarecrow, a Tin Man, and a Lion. It takes thinking for ourselves (Scarecrow), opening our hearts to our passions and desires (Tin Man), and having the courage to make the choices that set us free (Lion). I am reminded of a paragraph from a goodbook, called Spiritual Journeys Along the Yellow Brick Road by Darren John Main:

So here in this moment, each one of us is presented with a choice – the only choice there ever was, and the only choice there ever will be. We can muster up our wisdom, compassion and courage and click our heels, or we can stand here looking up at the sky waiting for some external wizard to zip us off in a balloon filled with hot air.

Dorothy's mantra was, "There's no place like home." She focused on it, said it three times, and felt the feeling of 'home'. And that's where she went.

My mantra is, "There's no place like whole."

Becoming myself was a yellow brick road kind of journey that led me to discover, love, embrace, and express who I really am. The whole of me.

I hope you become your own biggest fan.

CPSIA information can be obtained
at www.ICGtesting.com
Printed in the USA
LVHW052313240723
753137LV00004B/193

9 781035 808274